Auguste Escoffier

Memories of My Life

To Cathy and Jeff,

Thank you for a memorable evening at Manresa with such good friends! I think you'll both enjoy reading this book — A bientôt en France, I hope —

Bien amicalement,

Michel A. Escoffier

Los Gatos, March 2007

Auguste Escoffier, c.1872

Auguste Escoffier

M e m o r i e s   o f   M y   L i f e

Translated by
Laurence Escoffier

Foreword by
Ferdinand E. Metz

Preface by
Pierre P. Escoffier

Introduction by
Julia Child

Van Nostrand Reinhold
I T P® A Division of International Thomson Publishing Inc.

New York • Albany • Bonn • Boston • Detroit • London • Madrid • Melbourne
Mexico City • Paris • San Francisco • Singapore • Tokyo • Toronto

Van Nostrand Reinhold Staff

President: Marianne J. Russell

Vice President, EDP: Renee Guilmette

Publisher: Melissa A. Rosati

Project Development Editor: Joan Petrokofsky

Assistant Editor: Amy B. Shipper

Editorial Assistant: Jill Elias

Manufacturing Director: Louise Kurtz

Editorial Production Director: Stephen McNabb

Senior Production Editor: Jacqueline A. Martin

Production Assistant: Carolyn Holfelder

Art Director: Mike Suh

Marketing Manager: Mary Fitzgerald

Marketing Associate: Michelle Agosta

Support Staff: Karren Abrams, Paul Aljian, Ginsen Chang, Dionicia Hernandez, Laura Morelli, Maria Menechella, Andrea Olshevsky, Madeline Gutin Perri

Photo credits: Unless otherwise credited, photos courtesy of Fondation Auguste Escoffier, Villeneuve Loubet, France

Copyright © 1997 by Van Nostrand Reinhold

I(T)P® an International Thomson Publishing Company
The ITP logo is a registered trademark used herein under license

Printed in the United States of America

For more information, contact:

Van Nostrand Reinhold
115 Fifth Avenue
New York, NY 10003

Chapman & Hall GmbH
Pappelallee 3
69469 Weinheim
Germany

Chapman & Hall
2-6 Boundary Row
London
SE1 8HN
United Kingdom

International Thomson Publishing Asia
221 Henderson Road #05-10
Henderson Building
Singapore 0315

Thomas Nelson Australia
102 Dodds Street
South Melbourne, 3205
Victoria, Australia

International Thomson Publishing Japan
Hirakawacho Kyowa Building, 3F
2-2-1 Hirakawacho
Chiyoda-ku, 102 Tokyo
Japan

Nelson Canada
1120 Birchmount Road
Scarborough, Ontario
Canada M1K 5G4

International Thomson Editores
Seneca 53
Col. Polanco
11560 Mexico D.F. Mexico

1 2 3 4 5 6 7 8 9 10   QEB-FF   01 00 99 98 97 96

Library of Congress Cataloging-in-Publication Data

Escoffier, A. (Auguste), 1846-1935
   [Souvenirs inédits. English]
   Auguste Escoffier, memories of my life / by Auguste Escoffier; translated by Laurence Escoffier.
       p. cm.
   Includes bibliographical references and index.
   ISBN 0-442-02396-0
   1. Escoffier, A. (Auguste), 1846-1935.   Cooks—France—Biography.   I. Title.
TX649.E8A3—dc20   1996
641.5'092—dc20   96-25141
[B]   CIP

http://www.vnr.com
product discounts • free email newsletters
software demos • online resources

email: **info@vnr.com**

A service of I(T)P®

Contents

Foreword

I WAS INDEED FLATTERED when Michel Escoffier asked me to write the foreword for the English edition of *Memories of My Life* because the name Auguste Escoffier has always been, for me, synonymous with leadership and dedication, qualities which enabled this great master to almost single-handedly change the image and working conditions of the modern chef.

When I joined the Culinary Institute of America, I found similarly strong reverence for Escoffier, one that was deeply rooted in our teaching philosophies and was present throughout our curriculum, mandating an understanding of the importance of discipline and uncompromising attention to basic principles. Above all, Auguste Escoffier's love for the profession and his passion for cooking are the key elements that we hope to pass on to every one of our students. Our Escoffier Restaurant, the Escoffier Chair Award, and the Auguste Escoffier Alumni Awards serve as constant reminders of the values and qualities which his legacy represents to us.

However, no matter how much you think you know about Auguste Escoffier, it isn't until you read his own words that you begin to understand the man himself. Such is the case with *Memories of My Life*, a work that gives us a glimpse into all that made Auguste Escoffier the tireless innovator, the consummate teacher, and the quintessential chef.

Often called the king of chefs and chef of kings, Auguste Escoffier reminds us constantly to project a professional image and to advance beyond the obvious boundaries of the kitchen—seeking knowledge of service, understanding the importance of ambiance, gaining an appreciation of wines, and establishing contacts with our customers. Not only did he preach this, but even more importantly he personally set the example through his partnership with César Ritz at the Savoy and later at the Carlton hotels in London.

He was at ease with and enjoyed the admiration of the aristocratic, artistic, and scientific communities of his time. Almost in contrast to that, he was a champion of the ordinary cook and through his intervention transformed the culinary trade into a profession which brought us stature, recognition, benefits, and rewards.

His vision and inventive genius are well chronicled by reports of the extraordinary feats during his time in the army, as well as of his glorious reign as the executive chef at the Savoy and Carlton hotels.

As an advocate of human rights and a great supporter of many charitable organizations, it was, perhaps, Escoffier who stimulated today's chefs to embrace the concept of helping those members of society who are less fortunate than us. His vision of creating a chef's federation—a dynamic network within the culinary profession—has contributed immensely to the cross-continental movement of chefs which has brought over 2,000 French chefs as ambassadors to kitchens around the world.

One of his greatest contributions was the codification of cooking in *Le Guide Culinaire* through which he brought structure, discipline, and organization to a disorganized and chaotic workplace that, up to that point, barely functioned. After Escoffier's death in 1935, Joseph Donon continued the Escoffier legacy in America with the support of Les Amis d'Escoffier and Les Dames d'Escoffier which he established for that purpose. In France, Donon created the Escoffier Foundation and its Museum of Culinary Art which attracts visitors from around the world.

In reading these memoirs it becomes quite clear that Auguste Escoffier embraced life to the fullest as he made each day a significant and valuable learning experience. He taught us that each day was just a milestone along the journey of lifelong learning—a journey which, for us, begins with the teachings of Auguste Escoffier.

Ferdinand E. Metz

President
The Culinary Institute of America

Preface

After the death of Auguste Escoffier in 1935, his son Paul, my father, gathered together all the documents and archives that were to be found between his house in Monte Carlo, his family residence since 1890, and his pied-à-terre in the rue Boissy d'Anglas in Paris.

In these archives, arranged chronologically, were found the memoirs he had already written, intended, as he specified, especially for those in his profession. Other documents, letters, articles, and reflections completed a testament spreading from the last years of the Second Empire to the great crisis of 1929 (including the Franco-Prussian War, the Edwardian Age, World War I, and the 1920s).

From 1935 to 1940, the French public was little inclined to be interested in culinary and gastronomic matters. Their minds were preoccupied with current financial problems, the consequences on daily life of Front Populaire legislation, and the worries caused by a war that threatened to break out at any moment.

Our memoirs remained untouched, but not forgotten.

After World War II and the years of occupation, the serious commitments of the post-war era pushed secondary and less-important questions to the background. At the end of the war we returned to our respective activities, which absorbed all of our time.

A generation passed before the public interest in the pleasures of fine food and culinary literature reappeared. This interest slowly took on unforeseeable dimensions, on both sides of the Atlantic.

The name of Auguste Escoffier had remained remarkably familiar and widespread, not only in France, but the world over. In France, the Fondation Auguste Escoffier and the Museum of Culinary Art, located in his childhood home in Villeneuve-Loubet, greatly contributed to the revival of his popularity.

If he remains, for his family, the most benevolent, understanding, and encouraging grandfather that anyone could hope to have, nevertheless there are few left today who have an idea of the kind of man he was and the reason for his fame.

My cousin Marcel Escoffier and I reread the documents our grandfather left behind, and the notes he had written about his life and career, and it seemed to us that it would not be out of place to publish them. We knew that his impressions of the periods that he lived through, the changes in which he participated, and his reflections on the culinary profession and the spread of French cuisine throughout the world could only be of great interest.

These memoirs were thus published in French in 1985. For this undertaking I must express my gratitude to Juliette Delannoy, whose encouragement and participation in the compiling of these documents were infinitely helpful, to Jeanne Neyrat, whose family documents helped to enrich the introduction in the original edition, and finally to Jeanne Lafitte for the interest she showed in this book and its original presentation.

As the name and reputation of Auguste Escoffier remain cornerstones of the culinary world, we decided that it would be of interest to publish an English translation of these memoirs.

The occasion of the 150th anniversary of Escoffier's birth on October 28, 1996, and the events planned worldwide to celebrate it encouraged my French-American daughter-in-law, Laurence Escoffier, to undertake this translation. My son Michel approached Van Nostrand Reinhold in New York with the manuscript, and their immediate interest helped to carry the project through. The English language version of the memoirs has been expanded to include some other archives that we found concerning Auguste's trips to the United States and notes to more fully explain the times in which he lived.

I wish to thank Laurence for her extensive work on this publication, and our editors for their enthusiasm and support, as well as Ferdinand Metz, President of the Culinary Institute of America, and my dear friend Julia Child for providing their opinions of the impact that my grandfather Auguste Escoffier had and still has in the world of culinary art.

Pierre P. Escoffier

Julia Child on Escoffier

Interview by Alexandra Leaf

Alexandra Leaf is a culinary historian and a member of the
faculty of the New School for Social Research, where she
teaches culinary history. She is the author of *The Impressionists'
Table: Recipes and Gastronomy of 19th-Century France.*

THE FOLLOWING INTERVIEW took place on the afternoon of July 12, 1996, in Julia Child's kitchen in Cambridge, Massachusetts. Over a delightful lunch of quiche Lorraine and "salade verte," we chatted about Escoffier while sipping glasses of crisp white wine. Julia Child never actually met Auguste Escoffier; when he was in New York, she was in California, and by the time she arrived in Paris, he had already passed away in the south of France at nearly ninety years of age. But France was still very much under the great chef's influence when Julia discovered the pleasures of the French table and "came of age." Although their concerns in many ways differed, both individuals, extraordinary in their own ways, were passionately dedicated to teaching people about and perpetuating the venerable tradition of *la cuisine française.*

What is the place of Escoffier today when we consider the nouvelle trends in French cooking with Asian or Latin American accents?

I think when you read Escoffier's introductions [to *Le Guide Culinaire* and *Ma Cuisine*], you see he had very contemporary ideas. When he was writing about sauces like *espagnole* and *demi-glace*, he said that there would probably be simpler ways of doing things in the future. I think his idea was that cuisine has to adapt to the times. He also believed in cooking for the customers. Giving them what they wanted. I'm sure he would be very happy with many of today's trends, and he'd probably have been at the forefront with all kinds of "diet" type things that would be delicious to eat. I hate those phrases "diet foods," "heart healthy," and so forth. I have a feeling nowadays that some of the young chefs scoff at the rules, and feel that they're wonderful and macho and can make things up themselves. I think also after the kind of 1960s "revolution" people wanted to throw everything out and start again. That point of view still exists. But some people are beginning to turn back a little more to the classics; it depends on how much education and training they've had. As André Soltner says, "We spent several centuries developing that splendid edifice *la cuisine française*, and there's no reason to throw it over."

Where and when did you first hear about Auguste Escoffier?

I suppose it was after I got married and started to cook. That was in the forties. I began with the *Joy of Cooking* and *Gourmet* magazine. Of course I had heard about Escoffier then. I think most people knew about him anyway. I must have gotten my first copy of *Le Guide Culinaire* at that time. Of course later, at the Cordon Bleu [in Paris], I heard much more about Escoffier.

During those early years in Paris when you studied at the Cordon Bleu, a young contemporary of Escoffier's, Max Bugnard, was your teacher, your maître. Would you describe that period?

As soon as we got settled in Paris, I went to the Cordon Bleu. At that point, their main thrust was classes for housewives. But I wanted more professional training. Fortunately, I was able to go down into the cellar where there was a wonderful old chef, Max Bugnard, and a bunch of GIs because at that point, if you'd been in the war, you could have two years of schooling free. What drove me into French cuisine was the seriousness of the art. I'd been looking all my life for something that really turned me on. Bugnard was so passionate about his art. I remember we hired him and his sous chef to do a birthday dinner for my husband, Paul. The menu doesn't sound that spectacular nowadays, but for us, in modest financial circumstances, it was marvelous. We began with sautéed foie gras, and then had a perfect tenderloin of beef with out-of-season asparagus—a rare occurrence in those days. For dessert, we had a beautiful chocolate mousse cake from one of the fine patisseries, and delicious wines from Nicolas [wine merchant]. Oh, yes, and I remember a dish we made with Bugnard at the Cordon Bleu. It was a ham mousse that took at least two hours to make. There were no electrical aids at that time, only elbow grease. To grind the ham, we used a huge, old-fashioned marble mortar. It must have been two feet across and two feet high and came with an enormous wooden pestle. When the ham was pounded into a fine purée, we pounded in egg whites and cream and stirred the mixture over ice. Then we rubbed it with a *champignon* [wooden pusher utensil] through a giant sieve called a *tamis*, and scraped it off the bottom of the sieve with a *corne* [tortoise-shell utensil]. The mousse was absolutely delicious, of course. Bugnard was a wonderful showman, yet very precise. And he had all the right classical ways of doing things.

Everything was classical in French cuisine at that point. There was none of this "creative cooking" that we find today. You went to a restaurant because it did, say, an excellent blanquette de veau, or lobster dish. You followed the rules.

What happened to Escoffier's legacy once chefs like the Troisgros brothers, Roger Vergér, and Paul Bocuse began introducing "nouvelle cuisine"?

It was in the seventies when the cover of a French magazine showed this big fat fellow dripping with gravy. And it said, "Down with Veal Stock" and so forth. And that was the clarion call to nouvelle cuisine. From then on, things changed a lot. Whether or not they're going back to a modern version of the classics, I don't know. I think chefs also have to bow to people's tastes as Escoffier realized he had to do.

I don't think the French are doing as much about no fat and no cholesterol as we are.

Who is Escoffier to you? Was he in any way an inspiration for Mastering the Art of French Cooking?

Escoffier is the master of "La Cuisine." A father of tremendous importance. I have great admiration for him. Of course he inspired us because we learned in the classic mode. He was an inspiration to our book because we wanted to do things the right way. But we were concerned with the home cook—the hobbyist middle-class cook. I think our book has very much the same point of view as *La Cuisine de Madame Saint-Ange* because the author of that book was interested in *la cuisine bourgeoise*, and so were we.

Of course, Escoffier was a professional chef speaking to restaurant cooks, so our concerns were not quite the same.

It seems so apparent in both Le Guide Culinaire *and in* Ma Cuisine *that Escoffier was extremely committed to sharing his considerable knowledge with others. Could you comment on Escoffier as a teacher?*

Well, he had to teach his people in the kitchen. And he must have been a good teacher. If Escoffier were here today, he would probably be teaching at the French Culinary Institute in New York City.

Do you feel that Le Guide Culinaire *should be required teaching for students in culinary school? I know that in some institutes, it's only optional.*

Well, I wouldn't consider a program to be serious if it didn't teach Escoffier, or classic French techniques. What do these schools supply as a substitute? Their own book, I guess. I know certainly at the Cordon Bleu and at La Verenne he's required.

Escoffier is considered to be the first "famous" chef in the sense that he was accorded a status that chefs were normally denied. How do you think Escoffier would feel about the celebrity status that so many chefs today have achieved?

I should think he would be delighted because he really worked so hard to make the profession respectable. I remember in one of his writings he said to his chefs, "When you go out, put on a hat, and a coat, and a tie and look like somebody." Cuisine was an art form for Escoffier.

What do you consider to be Escoffier's greatest contribution?

Making the art of being a cook respectable. Escoffier came from a modest background himself, so he was very much interested in being seen as having a serious profession. He had the highest standards for the quality and perfection of his food, and at the same time, he was very concerned with the atmosphere of the kitchen. He did a lot in terms of improving not only his cooks' attitudes in the kitchen, but also their conduct, because back then cooks often used to be drunken and dirty. A significant contribution that the CIA [Culinary Institute of America] has made is to give people pride in their profession. The school has also stressed the importance of running a clean, hygienic, sensible, safe kitchen—the proper environment in which well-trained chefs can produce splendid food.

Julia Child

Julia Child

P a r t O n e

First Experiences

1 8 4 6 – 1 8 7 0

Childhood Memories
Villeneuve-Loubet

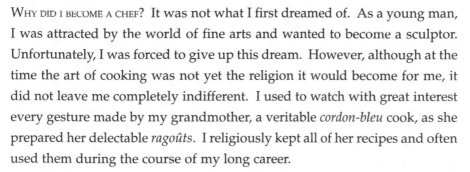

WHY DID I BECOME A CHEF? It was not what I first dreamed of. As a young man, I was attracted by the world of fine arts and wanted to become a sculptor. Unfortunately, I was forced to give up this dream. However, although at the time the art of cooking was not yet the religion it would become for me, it did not leave me completely indifferent. I used to watch with great interest every gesture made by my grandmother, a veritable *cordon-bleu* cook, as she prepared her delectable *ragoûts*. I religiously kept all of her recipes and often used them during the course of my long career.

My first experiment with cooking dates from 1856. I was ten years old and had no idea at the time that I would one day become a chef. In those days, coffee was not a common beverage; one treated oneself to this stimulating concoction only in certain circumstances. One morning, before she left for Nice, I watched my grandmother prepare coffee for herself in the traditional way. I waited for her to leave and then faithfully repeated her procedure so that I too could taste this coffee that I had heard so much about.

Some time later, I heard a group of women discussing ways of making coffee. The conversation took place at an evening gathering at our home, in front of a warm fire, and each lady had her own version. When they had all finished giving their ideas on the subject, I announced, "It really doesn't take much to know how to make coffee!" and told them about my small sin of curiosity. At first they scolded me a little, but in the end they all laughed, and my grandmother kissed me and whispered in my ear, "You'll make a good cook!"

At about the same age, it was my responsibility on Sunday mornings to look after the house of my maternal grandfather, as he was very elderly and lived alone. I would tend to his fire while he went out to Mass. I had often heard of a delicacy consisting of a slice of toasted bread that, while still piping hot, was spread with a particularly strong cheese, a kind of *pâté* called *brousse*, which was very much appreciated by the village folk. As there was plenty of this cheese at my grandfather's house, it was easy for me to satisfy both my curiosity and my gourmandism. Crouched in front of the fire, I pulled a small quantity of glowing embers onto the hearthstone and used the fire tongs to toast two slices of bread. Immediately I spread them with the famous *brousse*, and then reverently savored my cheese toasts, accompanying them with half a glass of sweet wine.

* * *

Nice and Savoy were returned to France by Victor-Emmanuel, King of Piedmont, in exchange for French assistance in the reunification of the Italian states, in 1860.

I was born on October 28, 1846, in the village of Villeneuve-Loubet (located in the department of the Var at the time, but now in the Alpes-Maritimes due to the reunification of Nice with France). I was the son of Jean-Baptiste Escoffier and his wife Madeleine Civatte. My father, like his father, practiced the trades of blacksmith, farrier, locksmith, and maker of agricultural tools. In short, local farmers never had to leave the village to obtain what they needed for their work.

My grandfather, Augustin Escoffier, completed his apprenticeship as a blacksmith, toured France as a journeyman, and fulfilled his military duties as Grenadier of the Guard during the last few years of the First Empire. He

was badly injured in battle when a bullet pierced his chest. After completely recovering from this injury, he returned to his village, got married, and
founded his own blacksmith's shop. His wife gave him five sons and one
daughter.

My father, the eldest of the boys, learned the profession of blacksmith.
The second son, François, became a cook, as did the third son. The fourth
son, Honoré, started off in his father's footsteps, but after his tour of France
as a journeyman, he returned home to the village, gave up his profession of
blacksmith, and became an innkeeper. The fifth son, Victor, showed himself to be very skilled in the art of working iron and was artistically talented. He was learning the ironworking profession when the Crimean War
broke out in 1855. Called into the army, Victor died in Constantinople of a
disease contracted while fighting the enemy. His sister, the youngest of the
family, married an Italian, Auguste Decaroly, owner of the Café des
Colonies, in Nice.

At the time of my birth, my father had to take over the management of
the smithy because my grandfather was suffering from a long illness.
Slowly, my grandfather's health returned, and he was able to enjoy a peace-
ful life until he died in 1871 at the age of eighty-four, leaving nothing but
affectionate memories of him in the region.

Although his formal education had been limited to primary school, my
grandfather's country upbringing had given him very high ideals. I remember that when my brother and I were children, my grandfather taught us to
be polite in all circumstances, to behave well at the table, and never to speak
to a lady without uncovering our heads. He taught us that *savoir-vivre** was
of the utmost importance in life. I have always remembered his precious
advice and often used it to good advantage.

When my father was a child there was no schoolteacher in Villeneuve-
Loubet, but the village priest, a charming and devoted man, enjoyed teaching his choirboys, including my father. My father in turn taught what he
had learned to all the young children of the village, giving them lessons
throughout the long winter evenings. His goal was to teach them reading,

* Savoir-vivre: proper manners, poise, and diplomacy. [ed.]

writing, and basic arithmetic, so that the young men could write to their parents or their fiancées without being forced to depend on the services of a stranger during their military service, which lasted seven years at the time.

My father died in his eightieth year. Like his father, he had always been ready to do the right thing, and was liked and sorely missed by all who knew him.

Early Beginnings
Le Restaurant Français

IN 1856 MY UNCLE FRANÇOIS opened a restaurant in Nice called Le Restaurant Français; it was located across from the public park on the corner of the rue Paradis.

In 1859 I was thirteen years old and had just celebrated my first Holy Communion. I was informed that I was to be a cook, and I was given no option but to obey. So I went to work for my uncle as an apprentice in October 1859, a year before Nice became part of France. A short time later the restaurant moved from the corner of the rue Paradis to 7 quai Masséna, and it was there that I completed my apprenticeship in 1863.

These were difficult years, but my desire and firm resolve to succeed helped me to accept the situation without the slightest outward manifestation of unhappiness. In just a few months, I had already realized the importance of cooking and the significant role that a conscientious cook could play in life.

* * *

In these days, working conditions in professional restaurant kitchens were very hard, rough, and physically demanding, especially for apprentices who occupied the lowest grade in the hierarchy. Escoffier's uncle showed him no favoritism. He was bullied, slapped, and shouted at just like everyone else, even though he was so small that he had to wear special platform shoes so as not to burn his face at the range.

At that time, high society held little esteem for the profession of cook. This should never have been the case, for cooking is a science and an art, and one who puts all of his heart into satisfying his fellow man deserves recognition. For too long the kitchen chef has been ranked among domestic servants. While it is not at all my intention to form the slightest criticism of house servants, it seems natural to make a distinction without dishonoring anyone. This distinction already existed during the Monarchy, when the *chef de cuisine* was ranked an Officer of the Crown, and enjoyed the most outstanding privileges. It is doubtless due to this tradition that noblemen have always held the fine art of cooking in special regard and do not consider it demeaning to make good food a true passion.

Indeed, there has never been a lack of chefs among the aristocracy. As his mother, Princess Palatine,* tells us in her letters, the French Prince Regent, Philippe d'Orléans, learned to cook in Spain when he was in command there. He liked to exercise this skill in Asnières, at a farm belonging to the Countess de Farabère. Every night the Regent would go to Asnières incognito, and it was a wonderful sight to see the nephew of Louis XIV preparing a hasty meal, a cotton apron protecting his silk trousers. Later he would dine with the Countess in the company of the farm peasants, singing cabaret songs, indulging in mad extravagances, and womanizing outrageously. Even at the Royal Palace he would sometimes amuse himself by preparing *ragoûts* for his fellow rakes, who would naturally not hesitate to shower his Royal Highness with compliments.

Louis XV, in the first years of his youth, loved to cook in his private apartments. When he grew older he remained very skilled at preparing *café au lait* for his mistresses.

If Madame de Montespan[†] had not known how to cook with such talent, would she have had such a grand destiny? A woman with such an understanding of food and wine is capable of enslaving the greatest kings on earth.

---

* Princess Palatine was the wife of Philippe I, Duc d'Orléans, the brother of Louis XIV. She wrote many letters home that recounted life at court and meals at Versailles. [ed.]

† Madame de Montespan (1640–1707), born Françoise-Athénaïs de Rochechouart, was a favorite of Louis XIV. [ed.]

The Duchess of Burgundy was renowned for a delicious concoction of vinegar and sugar that she served over boiled beef.

Montaigne wrote, "Nobles imagine that they know how to prepare fish." Indeed, fish was a luxury, and great lords enjoyed preparing it themselves. Fish was in vogue for ceremonial dinners. Even highly placed church officials impatiently waited for the season of Lent so they could fully enjoy feasting on it. At the royal court, fish was used in gambling games. Madame de Sévigné writes, "So-and-so lost a hundred *louis d'or* worth of fish." One abbot died after eating too much fish at the home of the Duke de Saint-Simon, who wrote in his memoirs, "The abbot of Verneuil died right after my arrival, and I was accused of having killed him with sturgeon that gave him such indigestion that he did in fact expire in my house."

Finally, if the Marquis de Béchamel had not invented his divine sauce, he would have been forgotten long ago.

But let me return to the subject at hand!

Having realized that there was, in the field of cooking, a vast domain to explore and develop, I said to myself, "Even though this is not the profession I personally would have chosen, since I am here, let me work to make the grade and do my best to improve the standing of the kitchen chef." This has always been my goal and I think I have given ample proof of my devotion to this cause.

I had barely had six months of training or experience when I became interested in writing menus. I started looking for words that sounded gentle and pleasing to the ear while expressing a connection with the food being proposed. All well-presented menus should be evocative, and increase the desire to partake of a skillfully prepared and presented meal. Menus for baptisms, marriages, and family celebrations are often saved. I thought these menus should reflect the occasion, as a sort of poem recalling the happy hours spent.

At about this time my uncle bought ten square English metal platters with covers; these comprised a setting for ten people. They were bought at a sale following the death of an English lord who had lived in Nice. I studied these very practical platters with great interest. I thought to myself, "If ever I open a restaurant of my own, this is the type of platter that I will have,

During the Ancien Régime, fresh ocean fish was only available for those willing and able to pay its high price, which included expensive transportation costs from the coast to Paris. Lakes and streams belonged to lords and monasteries; therefore, freshwater fish was unavailable to the general population.

Louis de Béchamel was a sixteenth-century financier, majordomo to Louis XIV. Saint-Simon described him as rich, a gourmet, and handsome, and reported that it was not likely that he himself created his namesake sauce Béchamel, but that it was probably an improvement of an older French recipe.

with a few modifications to facilitate the service, and in three different sizes." Long afterwards, the Hôtel Ritz in Paris gave me the satisfaction of realizing my dream. The company Christofle, responsible for the hotel's silverware, named my platters "Escoffier Plates." At first there was a small handle in the center of the platter's cover, which was fine for service in a private home but not at all practical for a hotel or restaurant. It was replaced by two little handles, one at each end of the cover, which also enabled the use of the cover itself as a platter in some circumstances, mainly for cold entrées.

My natural curiosity also encouraged me to look for anything that could develop and embellish the art of our national cuisine. My aim was twofold: to increase awareness abroad of French products and of ways to use them.

Nice and Monaco became fashionable winter destinations for Europe's nobility and moneyed class in the 1860s for several reasons. Queen Victoria had a villa in Menton, east of Nice, so the English aristocracy followed. In Prussia an 1858 edict against gambling led François Blanc, operator of a successful casino in Bad Homburg, to go to Monaco to develop what soon became the most famous and popular casino in Europe, especially after the completion of the railroad from Paris in 1865.

At that time, in Nice, Le Restaurant Français was the meeting place of high cosmopolitan society. The officers of the Russian Squadron who, every year, came to Villefranche to spend the winter season, were enthusiastic customers and fans of good food. To prepare some of their favorite national dishes, which they did not want to forget entirely, a Russian cook was included on the kitchen team. He enabled me to take notes that were very useful to me later on. At this time, Russian cuisine was very much in vogue in Nice, so I was delighted by such a happy circumstance.

During the summer season, Le Restaurant Français closed down from the end of May to September 1, and during that time I was in charge of cooking for the family. Our neighbor was a renowned confectioner and a pastry cook. The two chefs of these departments in his establishment very kindly invited me to visit them in their laboratory, and when I had a little free time I would take advantage of their kindness and help them prepare preserved fruits while learning about this branch of our profession.

Paris
Le Petit Moulin Rouge

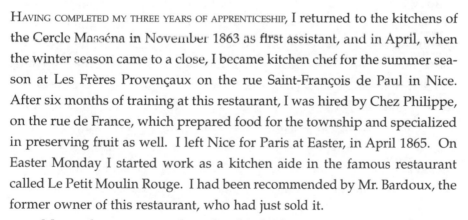

HAVING COMPLETED MY THREE YEARS OF APPRENTICESHIP, I returned to the kitchens of the Cercle Masséna in November 1863 as first assistant, and in April, when the winter season came to a close, I became kitchen chef for the summer season at Les Frères Provençaux on the rue Saint-François de Paul in Nice. After six months of training at this restaurant, I was hired by Chez Philippe, on the rue de France, which prepared food for the township and specialized in preserving fruit as well. I left Nice for Paris at Easter, in April 1865. On Easter Monday I started work as a kitchen aide in the famous restaurant called Le Petit Moulin Rouge. I had been recommended by Mr. Bardoux, the former owner of this restaurant, who had just sold it.

My readers may wonder what kind of restaurant it was. Le Petit Moulin Rouge was located at 19 avenue d'Antin, now called avenue Victor-Emmanuel.* There were garden groves in front of the restaurant, which consisted of two large dining rooms on the ground floor, two large rooms on the second floor, and several smaller rooms on the third and fourth floors —

* Today named avenue Franklin-Roosevelt. [ed.]

about thirty dining rooms in all. There was a private side entrance at 3 rue Jean Goujon, where clients could enter without being seen. This entrance was hidden by a huge roadside lilac grove, which vehicles could drive around. The greatest privacy was assured to every visitor.

This restaurant, which no longer exists today, was very much in vogue during the Second Empire. Members of French and foreign high society met at this fashionable cabaret on warm spring and summer days. It was not unusual to meet his Majesty the King of England, Edward VII, when he was still the Prince of Wales, dining in a private room with Gambetta and other political figures. At dinnertime one could find the most fashionable ladies in society as well as lovely Elisabeth, flower girl of the Jockey Club, offering her bouquets. Dinner was accompanied by the charming music of a perfect orchestra, the Concert Musard, located in the Champs-Elysées gardens just across the street from the famous restaurant, separated only by the avenue d'Antin. Today, part of the Grand Palais is to be found where the Concert Musard once stood, on the side bordering avenue Victor-Emmanuel.

The Jardin Mabille opened in 1844 and was an instant success, in part due to Monsieur Mabille's ability to attract influential members of society to his dance floor. The Jardin featured a long, gaslit gallery that opened onto a large garden; there, people danced around a central kiosk where the orchestra played.

At that time dinner was generally served between six and eight o'clock, and after a meal at Le Petit Moulin Rouge it was common to finish the evening at the Jardin Mabille, located nearby, at the beginning of the avenue Montaigne on the right-hand side. These two establishments, which for so many years shared their glory, were destined to have the same fate. In 1882, on the same day, at the same hour, an auctioneer's gavel came down to sound the knell of Le Petit Moulin Rouge and the Jardin Mabille, at a public auction of their equipment. Alas! Time passes, taking material things with it and delivering to the demolition crews those establishments marked by old age. In their place, superb new houses have been built, and nothing is left but the memory of their old names, unforgettable in the history of Paris.

I believe it will be of interest to my readers if I give them an example of the dinners we prepared at the time the restaurant was in its full splendor. Here is the menu of a dinner offered by the Count de Lagrande to his friends, to celebrate the victory of his racehorse, Gladiator, at the Grand Prix de Paris.

Melon Cantaloup Accompagné de Vin de Frontignan

• • •

Consommé Gladiateur au Suc de Tomates
Paillettes au Fromage

• • •

Truite Saumonnée au Coulis d'Ecrevisses
Pommes en Noisettes au Beurre Fondu

• • •

Selle d'Agneau de Behague, Sauce Soubise
Flageolets Nouveaux aux Fines Herbes

• • •

Blanc de Poulet en Gelée Printanière

• • •

Punch à la Romaine

• • •

Caneton de Rouen Bigarade
Coeurs de Laitues à l'Orange

• • •

Asperges d'Argenteuil

• • •

Pêches Impératrice Eugénie
Délices au Caramel

• • •

Café Mode Orientale
Grande Fine Champagne

• • •

Vins: Stamberger
Château Lafite, 1846
Veuve Clicquot (cuvée spéciale)
Château Yquem

The same evening, in a private dining room close to the one reserved by the Count de Paris, Cora Pearl could be found dining with a young lord, or perhaps I should say a young pigeon. This beautiful woman, who is far from forgotten, was particularly talented in the art of plucking these little birds so beloved by sensitive women. She took care to find them just as they left the nest, ready to fly alone, and then lavished her charms upon them until they were completely picked clean. Then, considering the deal closed, she turned to someone else. The Count D—— de Bouillon, then a young adolescent, must have kept the cruel memory of this heartless woman for a long time.

At the time, however, when this couple was sitting down to enjoy a *tête-à-tête* in front of an excellent meal, I proposed this appropriate menu to them:

Caviar Frais
Crèpes Mousseline
Melon Cantaloup
Fine Champagne

• • •

Un Léger Velouté de Poulet au Paprika Rose
Paillettes Pimentées

• • •

Petites Langoustes à l'Américaine
Riz au Beurre

• • •

Noisettes d'Agneau Cora Dressés dans les Coeurs d'Artichauts*
Petits Pois à l'Anglaise

• • •

Pigeonneaux† Cocotte
Coeurs de Romaine aux Pommes d'Amour

• • •

Asperges en Branches

• • •

Coupes aux Fraises
Gaufrettes Bretonnes

• • •

Fin Moka
Liqueurs

• • •

Vins: Bercastler
Château Lafite, 1848
Moët et Chandon

Cora Pearl, born Eliza Emma Crouch in 1842, was an English courtesan. She became one of the most successful and ruthless demimondaines of the Second Empire, extorting or cajoling huge amounts of money and jewelry from eminent clients. She was known for possessing a set of the finest horses and carriages in Paris. Zola's character in Nana (1880), Lucy Stewart, was inspired by this one-time mistress of Prince Napoléon.

Noisettes d'Agneau Cora

Cut *noisettes* from a lamb's neck, salt them lightly, sauté them in butter, and place them in freshly cooked artichoke hearts. Decorate with slices of truffle and lightly browned cock kidneys.

* In French slang, a coeur d'artichaut (artichoke heart) is a man who falls in love with every girl he meets. [ed.]
†Small pigeon; in French slang, a pigeon is a sucker. [ed.]

* * *

Among the most faithful customers of Le Petit Moulin Rouge was the Prince of R——, who came every Wednesday accompanied by a beautiful young lady. Their menu rarely varied. It generally consisted of soup, a lobster or crayfish *au court-bouillon* served hot with melted butter or mayonnaise, followed by an entrée of chicken or game, a Behague lamb roast, a vegetable, a dessert, and fruit. The lamb was rarely left out of the menu. One day I decided to accompany it with a tomato sauce *à la provençale*. This sauce pleased the prince and his charming guest so much that they never failed to request it thereafter.

Nearly three months later, the prince asked me for the recipe, as he could not find the equivalent anywhere else, and I gave it to him willingly. But when I mentioned that I included garlic in my recipe, his young lady friend sprang up as if she had just been personally insulted.

Upper-class disdain of garlic appears to date back to ancient Egypt. In the United States, it was not until the middle of the twentieth century that garlic became an accepted herb.

"What, sir? Do you mean to say you have made me eat garlic for the last three months? That's abominable! I hate garlic! I would have never expected to see it served in a first-class restaurant such as this one!"

The prince tried to calm her down, and I for my part tried to plead in favor of the use of garlic, finally winning her over to my point of view — thanks to my sauce! In the end the young lady conceded to our arguments, and ended up laughing at her own outrage.

Since then I have often had to uphold the cause of garlic in places or countries where it is held in inexplicable contempt. In antiquity, the Greeks hated it so much that people who had eaten garlic were refused entry to the temple of Cybele. Later, King Alphonse of Castile founded the *Ordre de la Bande,* whose members were sworn to eat neither onion nor garlic for fear of banishment from the Court. Let me assert that his great grandson, Alphonse XIII, has more sensible tastes.

I started to work at Le Petit Moulin Rouge in April 1865, but left in September 1866 to fulfill my military obligations in Villefranche-sur-Mer. My draft lottery number had classified me in the active army reserves, so I had only five months to serve. Right after these five months, I returned to Paris and on May 1, 1867 (the year of the World's Fair), I started work again at Le Petit Moulin Rouge, this time as pantry chef. The next season, in 1868, I was sauce chef. At the end of that season, I was hired as kitchen chef by the Count de North, bastard son of George IV, King of England, who, like his father, loved good food. However, the Count was obliged to leave for Russia in the early days of May, and I returned to my job as sauce chef at Le Petit Moulin Rouge in May 1870.

During the World's Fair of 1867, a large international crowd dined regularly at Le Petit Moulin Rouge. One evening at around seven o'clock, two carriages stopped on the avenue d'Antin, across from the entrance of the restaurant. A superb and impressive Arabian man stepped down from the first carriage, accompanied by three other persons; he was none other than the famous Emir Abd-el-Kader, the man who had for many years been at war with the French and had been their sworn enemy. In 1847, due to unfavorable events, he was forced to surrender to General Lamoricière, was imprisoned in Toulon, in Paris, and in Amboise, and finally was freed in 1858. Ever since then, he had proved a faithful friend of France.

Abd-el-Kader was hardly out of his carriage when he drew the attention of all the passersby. From the second carriage, four other Arabs in traditional dress joined him. Abd-el-Kader entered the garden of Le Petit Moulin Rouge surrounded by his followers, and created a sensation among the diners. Every eye was riveted to this vision of masculinity whose gaze was so piercing.

A table had been reserved for him and his guests in the Chinese Pavilion. From there he enjoyed an overall view as well as the lovely music of the Concert Musard. Here is the menu of the dinner that had been ordered earlier in the day:

Napoléon III and Empress Eugénie opened the 1867 World's Fair on April 1. A gigantic oval exhibition hall measuring five hundred by four hundred meters was constructed on the Champs de Mars to house exhibits for more than thirty nations, including the United States. The fair contributed to the international expansion of French cuisine through exhibits of its products and the more than six million visitors to the capital.

Melon Cantaloup Arrosé de Vieux Frontignan
Bisque d'Ecrevisses
Paillettes Diablées
• • •
Truite Saumonée Pochée au Vin de la Touraine
Sauce Mousseline
Pommes Bergerette
• • •

Selle d'Agneau de Behague Poêlée
Petits Pois à la Française
Laitues Farcies au Riz

• • •

Fricassée de Poulet à l'Ancienne en Gelée
Salade de Pointes d'Asperges Rachel

• • •

Aubergines au Gratin

• • •

Bombe Nélusko
Gaufrettes Bretonnes

• • •

Pêches et Raisins Muscats

• • •

Café Mode Orientale

• • •

Liqueurs
Grande Fine Champagne

• • •

Vins:
Champagne Parfumé à la Fraise des Bois
Château Yquem

After partaking of this excellent meal, Abd-el-Kader left the fashionable cabaret, surrounded once again by fascinated passersby.

In those days, every now and then I had the pleasure of attending wedding banquets, or simple lunches with friends, at the famous restaurant La Cascade.

In 1867 and 1868, Napoléon III transformed the Bois de Boulogne, still a wilderness at that time, into the veritable English park it is today. For several years, about 1,200 workmen labored under the orders of the engineer Alphand and the famous landscape architect Varé. Frequent alterations improved the original plans as time went on and new means of embellishment were discovered. The Emperor often visited the building sites, proposing new ideas. Even the Empress did not hesitate to use green watercolor to shade the map of the Grande Cascade. When the lakes were dug, the earth removed was used to create terraced borders, steep embankments, and gracefully sloping islets. A waterfall was built with rocks found during excavations when the park was laid out and with other big blocks that were brought in from Fontainebleau. Everything was held together by cement, and the result was that this waterfall, its cave, and the other artificial creations in the park all have a naturally wild and picturesque aspect that is a surprise and a pleasure to look at.

For a long time, the restaurant remained the goal of walks and strolls and the favorite stopping place for elegant carriages and dashing horsemen. At that time it was in its glory, welcoming the so-called *"cascadeurs"*— revelers, dandies, leaders in the world of fashion and exhibitions, etc. And it was the location of every important wedding reception.

Then came the bicycle. The restaurant became extremely crowded with a more democratic clientèle. But as the old gives way to the new, soon automobiles appeared. Their timid and audacious trial runs and frequent breakdowns at the racetrack heralded the restaurant's golden age. The beautiful horses, relegated to the background, soon disappeared in favor of the automobile, which could speed down endless roads toward different and often less attractive sites. Except on days when races are held at the Longchamp racetrack, La Cascade now seems to be too close or too far from Paris.

But time, happy or sad, marches on with long strides. These years witnessed the height of the French Empire, its worldwide prestige, the World's Fair of 1867, and the presence of European sovereigns in Paris.

Then came war and defeat, the terrible years of death and pain. When, in July 1870, the inevitable Franco-Prussian War broke out, I was immediately called to join my regiment.

Part Two

Rhine Army Chef

July – October 1870

Mobilized!

In 1870 I WAS WORKING AS SAUCE CHEF at Le Petit Moulin Rouge under the orders of Ulysse Rohan.

During the few days that preceded the declaration of war, Paris was in a strange mood. In general, people were ignorant of the hidden side of politics and the diplomatic intrigue surrounding the candidacy of a Hohenzollern to the Spanish throne, and took at face value the news (as false as it was absurd) that the French ambassador had been driven out by the King of Prussia. This supposed insult to France irritated everyone tremendously.

As a result, during the now-famous July 15 session of the National Assembly, there was absolute delirium when a majority vote broke off diplomatic relations with Prussia, based on the solemn and optimistic declarations of Field Marshal Le Boeuf and despite the objections and desperate efforts on the part of Thiers, Favre, and several others to counter the motion. Very few Frenchmen truly believed that the campaign would be any more dangerous than a simple military march followed by a triumphant

Ulysse Rohan was head chef at Le Petit Moulin Rouge, and like most of his contemporaries, he believed that it was impossible to govern a kitchen "sans une pluie de gifles" (without a shower of slaps). These were often delivered with little provocation, and usually to the newest or youngest member of the kitchen staff.

21

return, as the current expression went. How could anyone not believe in the success of our armed forces, considering the widespread affirmations of our supremacy at the time? Several newspapers published such headlines as "Let the Prussians take all the time they need — France is ready!" Those who believed this were no doubt well intentioned, but they were wrong, for future events soon proved that France was not ready at all.

Right after the declaration of war, the regiments of the Parisian garrison marched through the streets and boulevards of Paris, escorted by huge and enthusiastic crowds, to the railway stations where trains were waiting to take them to the border.

Enlisted in the Reserve Army with the class of 1866, I had served five months in the Twenty-eighth Regiment and had been assigned to the Third Infantry. The departure of the Parisian regiments signaled the imminent departure of the reserve forces. I soon received my call to the colors.

The day after France broke off diplomatic relations with Prussia, the War Ministry asked the Société des Cuisiniers de Paris to provide the names of a dozen chefs in the reserve army for assignment to various sections and services of the General Headquarters of the Rhine Army. Events followed so rapidly that this request went practically unheeded; the Société was able to provide the names of only a few men, who were sent to the Bonaparte barracks and immediately put to work in the kitchens there.

Time was of the essence, however, and under pressure from the Ministry, recruiting officers had to find the necessary chefs at once. As such I was hired at Le Petit Moulin Rouge by Colonel d'Andlau, chief of the Second Division, to be *chef de cuisine* of that division at the Rhine Army headquarters, with my friend Bouniol as first assistant. We were ordered to report to the Bonaparte barracks, where we found colleagues who had been appointed to various services, including my friend Fagette, who was assigned to the First Division.

I remember an incident that seemed unimportant at the time but which took on its full meaning four months later when I was a prisoner in Mainz: the departure from the Bonaparte barracks of the First Turcos Regiment,* headed by Colonel Maurandy. In the courtyard, the regiment

* Algerian infantry. [ed.]

was lined up in battle order. The Colonel stood straight in his stirrups, sword in hand, and cried out a vibrant "Forward, march!" To the thump of the drum major's stick rang out an old French marching song, sonorous, martial, inspiring, forcing new soldiers into step and making old soldiers proudly straighten their shoulders. The First Turcos Regiment was marching to the border! As they passed under the barracks' archway, the drum major turned around and, without missing a beat, cried out, "Take a good look at this door, my children! It may be the last time you see it!" As it turned out, the first soldier I met when I arrived at the prisoner's camp in Mainz was this very drum major. Alas, his prophecy was justified, for many soldiers in this heroic regiment had found death at Wissembourg.

* * *

The First Turcos Regiment left only a few hours before we did. In turn, we left Paris in the afternoon with the Sixth Cavalry, to which most Headquarters personnel had been assigned, and we were taken to La Villette. From there, a special train took us directly to Metz, where we arrived on the morning of July 25. Naturally, high spirits reigned during the trip and, so as not to lose the habit, we entertained ourselves by singing patriotic songs. In Metz we camped out on the rue Sous-Saint Arnoux and on the square in front of police headquarters until August 14. During that time I lived the life of a trooper and took care of the cooking needs of my fellow soldiers. Bouniol was immediately assigned to the officers staying at the Hôtel de l'Europe, in the capacity of *maître d'hôtel*.

On the morning of August 14, I began my official functions at the Second Division Headquarters.

Trial by Fire

ON THAT DAY, the Emperor, the Imperial Prince,* and their chiefs of staff left Metz in the afternoon, escorted by a hundred guards and a battalion of guides, to go to the army camp at Châlon.

They stopped at Moulin-les-Metz, and our division was ordered to leave Metz and join them. At the same time we heard heavy gunfire coming from the east; the battle of Borny had begun.

Our orders to break camp arrived so suddenly that I had just enough time to buy a huge joint of beef and some canned goods, which I quickly placed in trunks and loaded onto our wagon. Our particular convoy was made up of this wagon, loaded with the officers' trunks and supplies, pulled by two horses driven by a remount officer. The wagon bore the sign "General Headquarters, Second Division." We were allowed to ride next to

* The Imperial Prince Escoffier refers to was Napoléon's heir, who was born in 1856 and, had the Empire survived, would have simply succeeded him. [ed.]

24

the driver or walk alongside the wagon, but it was only on this one occasion, on September 1 during the battle of Sevigny, that we actually had access to it.

The soldiers assigned to the chiefs of staff and their wagon train were generally under the orders of a lieutenant, but I was the only one in charge of the wagon of my division, and I had the only key that opened it. Our usual uniform was naturally that of our regiment, but as soon as we stopped, we exchanged our tunics for kitchen jackets.

The road from Metz to Moulin was so crowded that it took us about eight hours to go four or five kilometers, and we arrived only at dusk. We were novices yet we set up our campsite with the speed and polish of real North African troopers. Our division's camp was on the outskirts of the village of Moulin, behind a little house near the construction site of the railroad line to Rheims.

It was about eleven o'clock at night, and I certainly had no desire to sleep. A constant feeling of uncertainty and especially the nagging worry about how I would provide the next day's menu were enough to keep me awake. It was a beautiful night, one of those hot, dry evenings so dear to the hearts of vagabonds and railway workers. Bouniol and I had stayed outdoors to discuss the problems we were going to have obtaining supplies in this region that had been completely pillaged by constant troop movements. I was especially concerned about how to use the joint of beef I had brought with me, an excellent piece of meat, to be sure, but which could hardly be eaten raw.

How on earth was I going to cook it? Should I braise it in the traditional manner? Impossible, as the enemy was all around us, and at any instant we could be ordered to break camp. I didn't want to have to abandon my *pièce de résistance* at any cost. A feeling of great danger leads to firm resolution, and my decision was quickly made.

"By God," I announced to Bouniol, "I am going to roast it, and right away. That way, whatever happens, we won't be taken by surprise, even if we have to break camp in the middle of the night." We started work right away, and the fact that necessity is the mother of invention was never so true as in the situation in which we found ourselves.

Four stakes were broken off the hedge surrounding the railroad yard and dug into the ground, crossed in the shape of an X about sixty centimeters apart to improvise the supports for my rudimentary spit. A fifth stake, squared off with a sword, served to skewer the animal, and the same hedge provided fuel. Five minutes later the spit, worthy of classical antiquity, blazed with light. This gave rise to such astonishment in the camp that we had many visitors. It would not have taken much to turn these curious spectators into a band of thieves. They were sorely tempted by the appetizing sight of the meat, which was just starting to roast nicely.

The scene soon turned Homeric, as Bouniol and I had to take up our swords to defend our property and repel the daring attempts made to abduct it. One of the trouble makers, a Zouave, overcoming our vigilance, crawled near and was even daring enough to stretch out a sacrilegious hand. Bouniol, in a fury, hurled himself at the aggressor and treated him to a generous sample of the curses contained in a soldier's vocabulary, which God knows is varied, while the Zouave shamelessly swore that he had only wanted to borrow a light for his pipe.

At seven o'clock the next morning, on August 15, we were ordered to have a full meal ready for nine o'clock, because the plans of the day made it uncertain as to when a second meal might be forthcoming.

I was proud of last night's decision and quickly drew up my menu, which was:

Sardines in Oil

• • •

Sausage

• • •

Soft-Boiled Eggs *

• • •

Roast Beef, Well Done

• • •

Potato Salad

• • •

Coffee

• • •

Fine Champagne

* I had been able to obtain eggs from a farm located 500 meters away.

We left Moulin in the middle of the day to go to Gravelotte, where we arrived around six o'clock. My first task was to set up my kitchen and send Bouniol out to find fuel and especially water, which was becoming very hard to obtain in this area, where there were so many thirsty men and horses. In normal times, and with the dry weather prevailing, the population of the village would have had just enough water for their own needs. By snooping around the village, Bouniol discovered a well that had not yet gone dry, but the farmer who owned it flatly refused to give him any water. Bouniol had to use more finesse in his arguments. "Fine," he said, "if you don't let me have a few liters of water, I'll go get all of my fellow soldiers and their horses, and then we'll see whether you can refuse them!" The frightened farmer agreed to give him some water, which was lucky because all the other wells in the village were dry. Had I not also had a small filter that I had bought quite by chance before leaving Paris, and which I used to filter several liters of muddy horse-trodden water, I would have been in a great deal of trouble. I am sure that on that hot day many men and horses suffered horribly from thirst.

I was finally able to draw up my menu, which included:

Tuna Fish

• • •

Sardines

• • •

Sausage

• • •

Onion Soup

• • •

Sautéed Rabbit

• • •

French-Fried Potatoes Cooked in Hot Lard

• • •

Cheese

• • •

Coffee

The rabbit that figured on the above menu surely merits a place in the annals of this military campaign, and could be called the *Lapin de Gravelotte,* not only because it was probably the last one existing in the region, but also because of the way it was prepared. Just to catch it we had to resort to all the wiles of Sioux Indians tracking down their prey. Then we had to find a way to cook it. Should we transform it into *boudin* sausage or cut it into cutlets? Quite unthinkable, as time was getting on. All things considered, I cut up my rabbit, sautéed the pieces in hot lard, and added six large onions that I had chopped finely. I sprinkled the lot with salt and pepper, a glass of cognac, the same quantity of white wine, and left it all to simmer. Twenty minutes later, the *lapin sauté* was ready to be served. (One could just as well have called this dish *lapin à la soubise*, as the principal flavor was from the onions rendered down to a purée in the cooking process.)

May I add that our officers found it delicious. Of course, they were men who normally were very fond of good food but who had learned to make do with little in these hard times, and they fully appreciated any effort made to satisfy their appetite. They had more serious worries than what they were given to eat, and their desire to fulfill their duty conscientiously and courageously was their major preoccupation.

Thus dined the chief officers of the Rhine Army General Headquarters on that evening of August 15, 1870, the day of Assumption, the day of Our Lady, patroness of France, and the eve of the Battle of Gravelotte, which would remain in history as one of the greatest of the century—the only one, unfortunately, in which our victory was without contest, making us forget our previous setbacks and filling our hearts with self-confidence and hope for the future.

Villeneuve-Loubet in the nineteenth century.

Auguste Escoffier, c.1900, at the Carlton Hotel in London.

Escoffier's father, Jean-Baptiste Escoffier (1822-1901), c.1890.

Delphine Daffis Escoffier, wife of Auguste Escoffier, c.1890.

Auguste Escoffier, c.1920.

Escoffier in Monte Carlo with his wife, Delphine (seated left); his son Paul (far right); his daughter Germaine (far left), and his grandchildren, c.1930.

*The house where Escoffier was born and spent his childhood in Villeneuve-Loubet, today trans-
formed into the Museum of Culinary Art by the Auguste Escoffier Foundation.*

"La Villa Fernand," Monte Carlo, Escoffier's family residence from 1885 to 1935.

The Battle of Gravelotte

THE NEXT DAY, very early in the morning, the Emperor and the Imperial Prince left Gravelotte for Verdun; Bazaine took command of the armed forces. The morning was beautiful, and nothing served to warn us that fighting would break out so shortly.

At 9:30 I was serving an outdoor meal to the officers, consisting, inevitably, of:

Hors d'oeuvre
• • •
Leftover Roast Beef from Yesterday
• • •
French-Fried Potatoes
• • •
Cheese
• • •
Turkish Coffee

The coffee had barely been served when the sound of gunfire put everyone on alert. Without even finishing their lunch, the officers jumped onto their horses to get to their posts, and a few minutes later the fighting began. It was to last until ten o'clock that night. At exactly the same time, on the other side of the village, my friend Fagette was serving coffee to the officers of his division. A regiment of armored cavalrymen appeared, and the officers invited its colonel to have a drink with them. The colonel stopped and joined the officers for some coffee, but at the moment he lifted the glass to his lips, he heard the first sounds of gunfire. He put down his glass and galloped off with his cavalrymen in a hurry. He was killed at the end of the day.

I cannot describe the different phases of this battle, as the thick of the fighting took place a few kilometers away from me, nor indicate which regiments moved in to take part in it. I can only report several events that happened near the place where we were stationed, behind a farm located on the road to Verdun, about five hundred meters from the position we had held that morning on the side of the hill facing Gravelotte.

On this farm a mobile hospital had been set up, and from the very beginning the injured poured in in droves. We were then able to see what war was really all about. Among the first to be brought in was a young soldier whose arm had been badly injured. He refused to let go of his rifle, whose barrel was twisted. I offered him a glass of rum to give him strength and helped him to the ambulance. On the way he told me he was a pastry cook and came from Aix-en-Provence; in short, he was a compatriot.

At around four o'clock, an emergency alert was sounded in our camp; about twenty men appeared on the top of the hill where we were stationed, backing down towards us and firing toward the opposite hill. We guessed that an enemy unit was advancing in our direction. A lieutenant was immediately dispatched to find out what was happening. Imagine his surprise to discover stragglers from various regiments who, shirking their duty both to the garrison and as soldiers on the field of battle, were using their ammunition to hunt hares that had been frightened out of their dens by the sounds of gunfire and were running about wildly on the hillside. Needless to say, the lieutenant did not exactly heap praise on the heads of these soldiers, and he immediately had them sent right to the front lines.

I would have gladly forgotten this incident, considering the dishonor it is for soldiers to think nothing of using their war ammunition on a hunting expedition, but I feel it necessary to underline their cowardice in the face of the courage of the other soldiers of the forty-third line who at the very same time were carrying out bayonet charges on the enemy. While the rabbit hunters were causing us such emotion, three cavalrymen, no doubt survivors of the charge against Bon Bredox's brigade and the Magdebourg cavalrymen, arrived at our makeshift hospital, both men and horses literally riddled with injuries. One, indeed, had had his nose blown away by a bullet. All three, in a state of incredible agitation, had themselves summarily bandaged and, having downed a glass of cognac, jumped back up on their mounts and spurred them on to battle, crying, *"Vive la France!"*

The fighting ceased at ten o'clock at night. The German army was pushed back in the direction of Ars-sur-Moselle and the harassed French troops took up their new positions for the night on conquered territory. The officers of our division straggled in one at a time, luckily safe, one and all, and I quickly prepared to serve them the dinner they badly needed.

The night was very dark, with such a strong wind that the candles lighting the outdoor tables were constantly being blown out. Bouniol expressed his frustration by swearing continuously like a trooper. Everyone was in high spirits and the officers told us an incredible tale of their near defeat.

In the middle of the battle, just as Marshal Bazaine was proceeding with his men to a battery that he had established, he was suddenly surrounded by several battalions of German soldiers. The easy victories that these Black Hussards had grown accustomed to had made them very daring without increasing their bravery. Like simple soldiers, the marshal's chiefs of staff drew their swords and charged the Prussians, who immediately scattered. If these Teutons had been really courageous, the marshal and all of his officers would surely have been taken. It even happened that Captain Tamajo, carried away with ardor, started chasing a fleeing German officer. He soon caught up with him, and they galloped abreast, striking and parrying with their swords until a soldier among our friends, named Hubert, under the orders of Colonel Samuel, galloped in from the opposite direction, drew his sword, and ran the German officer through. Both

Captain Tamajo and Hubert returned safely to headquarters, and a little later Hubert received military honors for his courageous intervention.

At two o'clock in the morning, the officers had barely finished eating when the order was given to return to Metz. We had to break camp and leave immediately in the pitch-black night. The day of August 17 was spent on a futile and tiring march that lasted until late in the evening, when we arrived in the village of Plappeville, situated under the fort of the same name, just west of Metz.

With the officers of the division, we were able to find lodging for the night in a small inn. General Headquarters had also been transferred there, with the accompanying battalions camping at the edge of the village. The next day, at around eleven o'clock in the morning, the sound of gunfire was heard, signaling the beginning of the battle of Saint-Privat, where Guillaume's grenadiers all found their deaths, as the old king telegraphed to Queen Augusta. German historians call this battle the Battle of Gravelotte.

It was also the last battle fought by the French forces in the countryside beneath Metz. The next day fighting was concentrated under the fort and around the walls of the town. The cannon fire, which intensified every moment, showed that things were serious. Officers came and went, anxious and worried, commenting on our chances for victory and thinking about many things other than their food. And yet I was able to provide a relatively comfortable meal that day, consisting of:

Hors d'oeuvre
• • •
Fried Eggs
• • •
Blanquette de Veau
• • •
Lamb Chops and French-fried Potatoes
• • •
Coffee
• • •
Liqueurs

But my menu had little success, as men's minds were otherwise occupied.

The *Pâtés* of the Siege of Metz

ON AUGUST 19, army movements had brought us between the forts and the town, where we spent the day and night. On the twentieth, we arrived at Ban-Saint-Martin, where Marshal Bazaine established headquarters in the villa Cornélis, where he was to stay until the surrender. The marshal's cook was a certain Mr. Perrin, the son of a Metz pastry cook who took over the Maison Chevet* established in Rheims a few years later. Ban-Saint-Martin is a sort of esplanade located at the very doors of Metz, about as large as the Place des Invalides. It was used for inspection of the troops and was surrounded by a circle of townhouses, villas, and tall poplars which were later cut down. The Zouaves camped there, along with the cavalry of the Guard and part of the artillery.

Our division was lodged at the home of Mr. Beaubourg, a Latin teacher at Metz's secondary school, who was very kind in putting his kitchen at my

* A famous French catering firm. [ed.]

disposal. As of that day, the first division of Army Headquarters, with Fagette as chef, joined our division, and we remained together until the surrender. We transformed a hangar at the bottom of the courtyard for our use as a dormitory, and we lodged there with the officers' orderlies.

On August 20, the Red Prince, heading seven army battalions, started occupying Metz, which, eight days later, after the battles of Noisseville, Nouilly, and Coiney, became an army stronghold. In both the military and civilian worlds, one idea dominated all minds: forcing the German lines and joining MacMahon's army, marching on to Montmédy. Everyone was persuaded that the two armies would soon unite. The possibility of a siege was not even mentioned. We could have ensured the town's supplies by bringing in wheat, fodder, wine, and vegetables that were still to be found in the suburbs of Metz, and this simple precaution would have avoided much future deprivation for the army and the civilian population. We could even have left plantations in the fields, at least in some cases, and harvested them later, but it seems that it pleased some to destroy and spoil these fields that would have been so useful.

The second and third army corps camped on the sides of Mont Saint-Quentin below the Plappeville fort. The various divisions of the army corps installed themselves in fruit plantations and vineyards and promptly devastated them, even though the grapes were not ripe at the time. This destruction became so serious that the commander-in-chief had to give orders to stop it by taking strict measures against offenders, who were condemned to ten months of confinement in the fort.

From August 20 to August 28, the army moved continually; orders were given and countermanded and plans were conceived and immediately abandoned. Everyone still believed in MacMahon's imminent arrival, which was celebrated in characteristic French style by such humorous forms of litany as "MacMahon, give us back our legs of mutton and tender steaks, etc." As of August 28, provisions were becoming rare, and horse meat appeared in the butcher shops. Eggs cost six francs a dozen, sugar over three francs a kilo. Fresh butter had disappeared. It had been eight days since the German army had surrounded Metz and already there was vague talk of rationing.

The siege of Metz was minor compared to the siege of Paris where, within one month, due to food shortages, horse meat was being sold at the market in Les Halles. Eventually, cats, dogs, and rats were served. And on the menus of fashionable restaurants, buffalo, antelope, kangaroo, and elephant meat, from the former residents of the zoo, inevitably appeared, as Parisians desperately sought nourishment.

* * *

Since our arrival in Metz, I had an inkling of what might happen, and took some precautions as a result. In a courtyard located at the bottom of a garden that only I could get into, I gathered together some fifty hens and chickens, several geese, ducks, and turkeys, half a dozen rabbits, two small pigs, a sheep and a goat. I also hid four large jars of Metz's excellent and famous plum jam, which later was of great use to me, as I was able to use it to replace sugar when it completely disappeared.

I put away about twenty kilos of salt, which came in very handy when it ran out in later days and desperate means had to be taken to replace it, such as using the salt water sources that supplied the tanneries, or resorting to chemical substitutes invented by druggists. Finally, I completed my reserves with a provision of sardines, marinated tuna fish, and Liebig tins of preserved food, a fortunate inspiration that caused no complaints from my officers, as they ended up being the best served of all the chiefs of staff, except for Marshal Bazaine himself.

As long as I could get supplies at the town markets, I took care never to touch the provisions I had set aside. They would not have lasted long had I not taken this precaution. On the contrary, I never missed an opportunity to buy suckling pigs, with which I made excellent *pâtés*, which I called *les pâtés du siège de Metz*.

Baron Justus von Liebig was a German chemist. In 1850 he produced the first meat extract and later a powder of concentrated stock. He laid the foundation of modern nutrition by demonstrating that living tissue was made up of carbohydrates, fats, and protein.

* * *

On September 1 I took part in the battle of Sevigny. The day before, we had received the order to follow our divisions and were taken to the island of Chambière, where we spent the night. The night was freezing and we suffered a great deal from the cold. In the morning a thick fog rolled in and at daybreak we were taken to a position under the Saint-Julien fort. This time, I could follow the phases of the battle, being stationed in front of the Saint-Julien fort next to an artillery unit, reinforced by a unit of the Grenadiers of the Guard. The battery had hardly been set up when it was caught in a cross fire between Prussian cannons and riddled with shells.

I did not see the officers of my division again until the next day at noon when, sheltered beneath the ramparts, I was quickly able to put together an improvised meal composed of:

Soft-Boiled Eggs
• • •
Beef Liver aux Fines Herbes
• • •
Cold Meat
• • •
Swiss Cheese

Napoléon III joined Marshal MacMahon's forces at the front to share the perils of war with his soldiers. Together they attempted to relieve Metz. The Prussian Army cornered them at Sedan on August 31 and the next day, after a brief battle, French resistance was broken. Napoléon attempted to die a hero's death at the front-line in the hope that the throne might be saved for his son, but he fell dishonorably into the hands of the Prussians. Marshal MacMahon was wounded and captured.

Military historians have already described the battle of Sevigny and its consequences. Let me add that gunfire was very heavy, and that it was the last time I left Metz until the end of the siege. In the evening, when we returned from our camp, we learned that rationing had begun. The next morning a decree from the Governor of Metz ordered all available milk cows to be delivered to the armed forces. But many complaints addressed to the Governor pointed out that it was imperative to have milk available for women and children, so enforcement of this decree was postponed for the time being.

On September 7, when the news of the Sedan disaster was confirmed, there was general consternation. On the same day the first postal balloons left Metz; their invention was attributed to Captain Rossel, the same man who several months later would become War Minister under the ill-fated Commune and later end his career in front of a firing squad in Satory. This postal service by balloon functioned regularly from then on. It was, in fact, our only remaining means of communication with France, separated as we were by the German lines. We wrote our messages, consisting of a few lines only, on thin pieces of paper similar to cigarette paper, giving our families news of our health. Then all of these papers were put together in a small package attached to a little balloon that was released to the winds with the following message attached: "Will the person who finds this package please give it to the nearest post office." Many of these messages arrived at their destinations, and the few words they contained brought some degree of hope to families worried about the fate of the loved ones they knew were besieged in Metz.

The Beginning of the End

ON SEPTEMBER 8 the Governor decreed that each regiment should choose forty horses from those suffering the most from fatigue and hunger and deliver them for army consumption. The cavalrymen who lost their mounts due to this operation were issued arms as infantrymen. As of September 10, horse meat was the only kind of meat available, as the few cows left were reserved for the sick.

On September 13 the bread ration was again diminished, from seven hundred to five hundred grams.

Now and then a few cavalry regiments that were still functioning tried to go out to forage for food, but what was available within the protection of the fort's cannons was quickly exhausted, and as of September 18, we were ordered to gather the leaves of certain trees to feed the horses.

Around September 15 the lack of food supplies began to be felt and I had to attack my reserve. From then on horse meat was the highlight of my menus, which consisted of horse stew one day, braised horse meat the next, macaroni horse meat the next, horse meat with lentils, with beans, with peas, etc. I must say that if the meat of "man's best conquest" was at that time not cooked with every possible sauce, then it was at least garnished with every possible kind of bean. But I was always careful to first scald the piece of meat and then cool it before cooking, to remove its bitter taste and render it more edible. It is easy to understand that this meat could not be very tasty, considering the starving condition of the slaughtered beasts and the fact that only those in the worst possible shape were chosen to be eaten.

Right from the start I was careful to be as economical as possible and still serve my officers a sufficient amount of food, keeping an eye out for future needs. Dinner menus were made up of a thick or thin soup followed by the main dish, a roasted fowl from my farmyard, salad, and fruit, and then coffee and cognac. There would have been nothing regal about this fare in ordinary times, but in the conditions we were in it seemed wonderful enough. Lunch was almost always made up of leftovers from the previous day. I reached new heights in the art of preparing leftovers that I am sure would have stupefied Baron Brice and quite a few of my other colleagues.

The personnel, consisting of Bouniol, Fagette, his assistant, and me, lived on the same level as the officers we served, creating superb gratins with bits of meat from the leftover carcasses mixed with crushed macaroni and several spoonfuls of Béchamel. From time to time, and on these days there was jubilation among the lucky diners, I was able to obtain with great effort and at great cost some small pike fished from the Moselle, which I made into fish cakes.

Most vegetables were impossible to find, and as of September 20, potatoes disappeared completely. When some grew again a little later, soldiers had to go as far as the enemy outposts to dig them up. As for fresh vegetables, I had only turnips, although I must say I have never seen any better ones. I prepared them in every possible way, and they were especially appreciated when they accompanied a duck from my farmyard.

Fortunately, some of my chickens were still laying regularly. I saved these eggs religiously, and they made up the first and the sweet courses of

Sunday meals. I served them soft-boiled or sometimes poached on a bed of chicory leaves, and often as not on minced horse meat with a tarragon sauce.

In early October, the ration of meat was brought down to 250 grams. It is true that it had been increased by the forced slaughter of the horses, but this meat, cooked without salt and served with a poor-quality bread, made for very poor nutrition for most of the men. They soon contracted dysentery, which claimed many victims among them, first at Metz and later in captivity. The lack of salt was certainly one of the biggest deprivations of the army and the civilian population.

* * *

Our officers, all being generally wealthy, donated to their orderlies the entire portion of their pay that they received in the form of food such as wine, brandy, biscuits, etc. I could have taken advantage of this, but I much preferred saving these products to offer to my old friends of the Twenty-eighth Regiment, who were profoundly touched and deeply grateful. One of them had brought me a Prussian rifle from Ladonchamps that I was going to keep as an army souvenir, but at the time of the surrender I had to get rid of it, and threw it into the Moselle River.

The army and civilian population of Metz really began suffering around October 10. At this time even my provisions were starting to diminish seriously. In my Noah's Ark, the goat was most useful to me, giving me as she did half a liter of milk every day. Of this small quantity of milk cut with water I made a *sauce Béchamel* (without butter, obviously), which was of infinite use to me. I also used the goat milk for sorrel soup and to cook rice, which was my principal dessert during the siege. This is where my reserve of plum jam came in handy, to make a dessert that I later baptized *riz à la Lorraine*. I made it as follows: I garnished the bottom of a mold with rice cooked in goat's milk without sugar, since there was none. On this first layer of rice I spread a thick layer of jam, then another layer of rice, etc. On the last layer of rice I sprinkled a little crushed army biscuit in lieu of bread-crumbs.

On October 20 the lack of supplies obliged me to make a final sacrifice. I had one suckling pig left that I killed, and perhaps never before had one pig been so celebrated, for I used it to make such a variety of foods that even the usually extraordinary expectations of rifleman Larricot concerning his daily fare were at last met. Sausages, *boudins*, and *crépinettes* were greeted with joy. Roast fillets were garnished with lentils and hams with white haricot beans. Cutlets helped me to make a substantial pilaf. Finally, a succulent terrine was made from the head and remaining parts, which had all been kept religiously.

These various provisions lasted until October 25 and on that day I was truly frightened to take the inventory of what remained.

On October 27, after the decisions made on the previous day by the High Council of War, General Jarras surrendered at the Château of Fescaty, where he negotiated the terms of surrender with Prince Frederic-Charles and General von Stichle. An article in the agreement specified that army officers could keep their orderlies with them, and, as would be seen later, many soldiers benefited from this agreement when they were sent into captivity. On October 28 the act was ratified, Metz was delivered to the Prussians, and every army soldier became a prisoner of war.

On the morning of the third day after the army's surrender, I bade farewell to my hosts, who were extremely sorry to see me go and who assured me of their warmest regards, and went to the Metz train station to be taken off to Germany as a prisoner of war. To get to the station, I had to cross all of Ban-Saint-Martin, and never will I forget the sad sight of the few skeletal horses, all that remained of what had been the magnificent division of the Guard, dying in pools of water and trying to rise with difficulty as I passed them. They turned eyes on me that could have been human in their ardent and vital supplication. To the very last one, they were condemned to die there, these noble animals who had carried their riders in the charge of the Plateau d'Iron against the cavalrymen of Magdebourg, the Royal Dragons, and the uhlans of Altmark. They too were martyrs, victims of cruel mankind that had brought such suffering to Metz.

Part Three

Defeat and Captivity

November 1870 – August 1871

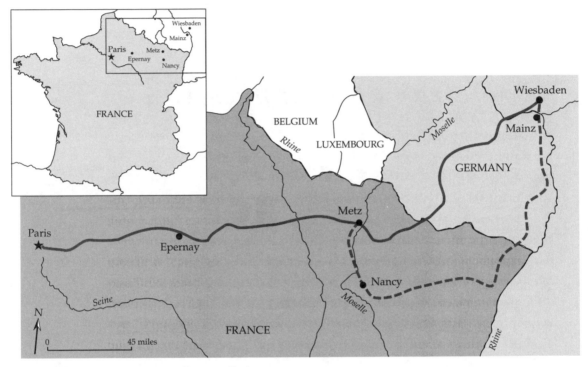

The railroad journey from Metz to Mainz and the return from Weisbaden to Paris.

Learning about Shame

On the third day after the French troops evacuated Metz, I resigned myself to going to the train station for transport to Germany. I was luckier than my fellow soldiers, and was spared the shame of having to march past the armed Prussian soldiers who lined the roads to supervise the columns of departing prisoners.

I was accompanied by Bouniol, who wanted to stay with me and was going to Mainz to join up with the lieutenant to whom he had been attached at the time of the surrender. Indeed, officers had been accorded the right to keep their orderlies during their period of captivity. I was assigned to the service of Colonel d'Andlau, and Fagette went to Hamburg with Colonel Levral.

Our relative liberty was explained by the fact that our officers were responsible to the Germans for our behavior.

* * *

A special convoy awaited us in the Metz station. We were hardly aboard when a strident whistle sounded, making us all jump, and the train pulled out of the station. We were on our way to exile, knowing only that we were headed for Mainz, but not knowing exactly where in Germany we would finally be interned. We stayed in the doorways as long as possible, waving in reply to the farewells addressed to us by the inhabitants of Metz. Soon the train rolled through the deserted countryside under a threatening autumn sky. Deep in our thoughts, we bitterly remembered that other train ride from Paris to Metz a few months before, when we had been so gay, so full of hope, and far from imagining this uninterrupted series of disasters.

Nancy was the first town where our train stopped. Access to the train station was guarded by the Prussian army to avoid the scandalous scenes that had marked the passage of the first few convoys of prisoners. Despite this precaution, and since the Prussian police could not help looking upon the agitators with some favor, stones were thrown on our train, and cries were heard, "Down with you cowards! Death to Bazaine! *Vivent les Prussiens!*"[*] May I hasten to add that the sounds of these drunken voices did not entirely echo with the French accent. Cowards? These soldiers who had fought so bravely? Who had been delivered to the enemy through treason rather than pure battle strength? Who had suffered so much, both morally and physically, and so many of whom had died far from home? Cowards? These men who had given up their arms in tears, and were now being sent into captivity?

Cowards? Yes, truly cowardly were those who could hurl such insults. They were worse than cowardly, this idiotically ferocious and criminal morass of men and women appearing from who knows where, every face reflecting hatred and ignominy. The women especially (I should say despicable females) in this ragged crowd were even more savage than the men. We spent a few truly atrocious minutes there, and we were very much relieved when the train pulled out of the station.

[*] "Long live the Prussians!" [ed.]

The Prussian soldiers did put up an appearance of trying to keep some semblance of order in this crowd, but it was obvious that in fact the demonstration enchanted them. What more could they hope for than to see French soldiers insulted in France by so-called Frenchmen?

* * *

We arrived in Mainz the next day at midnight; there had been no further incidents. The stations we passed on the way were full of troops, but even so, the German crowds which had gathered to see us pass spoke not one spiteful word.

It had taken us about four times the normal time needed to go from Metz to Mainz, probably because the Prussian train conductor had received orders to make the train advance at a snail's pace, but we figured it was neither the time nor the place to register a complaint.

As the Prussians were not legally held to take us in charge until Mainz, no food had been provided for us, but we were perfectly free to buy anything we needed at the train stops. At the final stop, everyone was free to go where he wanted and, as the inns were full, Bouniol and I were very happy to find a corner in a hotel's stable to spend the rest of the night.

The next morning, at the first light, I took advantage of the freedom we still had to circulate around town and find out as much as possible about how prisoners were treated. Unfortunately I did not speak a word of German and had to try to communicate with the Germans in sign language. Needless to say, these conversations in mime were of limited utility. To overcome this handicap, I bought myself a little French-German dictionary, and was soon able to get the information I was after.

A first disappointment awaited me. I was supposed to meet up with Colonel d'Andlau at Mainz. He had left Metz the first day of the surrender with several of our officers. However, they had been obliged to leave Mainz on the very day of their arrival, and I only found out later that they had been sent to Hamburg. The Colonel's orderly had been forced to remain behind in Mainz with his two horses. The poor young man was in trouble because he had no money. He had even had to sell one of the horses in order to feed himself and the other horse. This was a bad beginning, and Bouniol, who was exhausted, started complaining loud enough to break anyone's heart. It was not the right time for it, however, as we had to call upon all of our courage to get out of a sticky situation.

I thought the most important thing would be to find any kind of job at all, and I set about looking for one. I studied all of the main hotels in town, trying to judge from their outer aspect what their standing was and whether or not I should address myself to them. I finally decided to enter the Hotel d'Angleterre. The first person I saw was a young and charming maid. I asked her if she spoke French, and was astounded to hear her reply, "Alas, yes, I speak French, as I am Parisian, born in the rue d'Hauteville, where my parents are *concierges*." I was delighted to meet a compatriot and asked her everything I needed to know about Mainz, its surroundings, and also about Wiesbaden, where I knew many officers had been sent.

We spoke of home and of the sad events that had occurred, but soon, to my great regret, I had to bid farewell to this charming person. The unexpected encounter had cheered me up and, wasting no time, I continued my search. In the Ludovicsstrasse, I stopped in front of a superb pastry shop. A simple view of the goods offered convinced me that the establishment was a serious one, and I entered without hesitating. The owner received me in a way that made it quite clear that he had no love for Frenchmen. However, he answered that he might have some work for me.

As I was especially hoping to find work for Bouniol, and later figure out something for myself, I brought him over to the pastry shop the next day. An agreement was reached between the two parties right away, as this was no time to be too demanding. However, in all of this, we had completely forgotten that we were not free, but prisoners of war, and that in accordance with the general regulations, we needed the Governor's authorization to work in town. In fact, we had done everything backwards, and the proof of it was quick to come. We thought we would easily obtain this authorization when we presented ourselves at the desk, but not at all. To our bitter disappointment, we were refused without ambiguity, and sent back to the fort.

The German Canteen

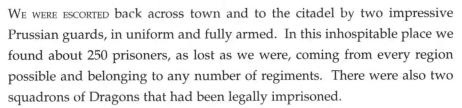

WE WERE ESCORTED back across town and to the citadel by two impressive Prussian guards, in uniform and fully armed. In this inhospitable place we found about 250 prisoners, as lost as we were, coming from every region possible and belonging to any number of regiments. There were also two squadrons of Dragons that had been legally imprisoned.

What can I say of the German canteen, installed in one of the buildings of the fort, aside that it looked much the same as ours? One ate a lot of sausage and drank a lot of beer…if one had any money. We got there on a Friday night and were assigned a big room to sleep in, located under the roof of the barracks, where there were some straw mats but no covers. The freezing cold made it an atrocious night. The next day we spent wandering around the courtyard, talking to each other and trying to figure out how we had managed to land in such a predicament.

On that day we had very little to eat. Keeping an eye out for the future, we contented ourselves with twenty centimes' worth of bread and sausage. A can of sardines that I found in my bag completed our provisions, along with an excellent glass of Château La Pompe.[*] The German authorities proved to be completely negligent. For three days they gave no food to the 250 prisoners enclosed in the citadel. If the Dragons had not shared their rations, the prisoners would certainly have starved to death.

Saturday night was spent in the same deplorable conditions. Finally, on Sunday morning, a trumpet sounded to call the Dragons into the courtyard for Mass. As we were mingling around with them, a German lieutenant asked us what we were doing there. A prisoner walked up to the officer and, saluting him, said, "Sir, why *are* we here? Excuse us if we ask you the same question. We have been here several days, completely left to our own devices, with no food at all. I don't believe it is your intention to let us starve, but if it is, I think it would be more humane to shoot us directly."

The officer spoke good French, and the soldier's brave words touched him. Luckily he was a noble man, and he immediately gave orders to take care of the situation. At two o'clock in the afternoon we were ordered to line up to march to a prisoners' camp situated on the plateau of Mainz, between the fort and the walls of the town.

It was upon my arrival there that I saw the drum major of the First Turcos Regiment, the same drum major who had called out to his drummers, "Take a look at this door, my children! It may be the last time you see it!" Without further introduction, and with the abruptness common in the military, I spoke to him about the departure of his regiment. He was going into town, where he had found work. I asked him to take a letter to the Ludovicstrasse pastry cook to explain why we had never returned to see him. I also asked him to carry a petition to the Governor on our behalf.

He did so, and with quick results. Three days later, Bouniol was able to leave the camp to work for our pastry cook making spice cake. I have already said that this pastry cook did not like the French and that he was prone to call us pigs, but I must add that he was not from Mainz, where most of the population did their best for the prisoners. His wife, for instance,

---

[*] A French pun, meaning "water from the pump." [ed.]

was a charming and agreeable person who did her best to make everyone forget her husband's vulgarity and brutality.

I cannot repeat often enough how the inhabitants of Mainz did everything to make our lot more comfortable, and when we were taken to Mass on Sunday, they often slipped us money, socks, and sweaters, even if they had to take great precautions not to be seen in order to avoid a blow from the rifle butts of the soldiers accompanying us.

* * *

Bouniol was finally taken care of, and I found myself alone in camp, where I had all the time I needed to study the variety of menus we were served, and especially to take note of the quality of the bread we received, which had the peculiarity of becoming edible two weeks after being baked. Every loaf therefore had the date it was baked printed on it.

The prisoners' daily fare consisted of one meal. One day it would be soup and red meat, the next old ham and rancid pork lard with lentils, split peas, or haricot beans thrown together with no care or cleanliness; it was not rare to find large white worms in this awful food. Even the beans, and especially the lentils, dug up for us out of the oldest stocks from the stores of Mainz, were never given the necessary soaking first, and were never fully cooked. It is probable that the next spring the owners of the fields surrounding our camp found themselves with a splendid crop of lentils coming from...guess where?

The soup was generally a potato, rice, or barley soup. It was edible the first few days of the week, but by Friday one needed to be starving to want to eat it. The reason is simple. Since potato was the vegetable generally used, an enormous quantity was needed, and every day a large team of about eighty men was assembled to peel one day's supply. These peeled potatoes were then thrown into huge beer barrels, and that was the end of the prisoners' work. The Prussians in charge of cooking contented themselves with throwing a few buckets of water into each barrel, which was hardly enough to clean five to six hundred kilos of potatoes! If all the potatoes had been used the same day, their cleanliness would not have been such a problem, but, in fact, for the first few days of the week the top layers were used, and by Friday, and especially Saturday, when all leftovers had to be used up, our soup became very heavy with the rotten potatoes taken from the fetid water in the bottom of the barrels.

Nobody thought to complain, however, as the difficulty we had receiving the mail from France worried us much more. With a little money, it was possible to get along in camp, but whoever had none suffered horribly. And at that time it took at least a month for anything to arrive from France.

The soup distribution was made every hour from 8:30 in the morning to eight and sometimes nine o'clock at night. It started on the right of the camp and proceeded by regiment. At this rate we received our pitiful ration only once every twenty-four hours, brought in from town on a wagon resembling those which come through Paris every morning to pick up waste water and garbage.

One thing I could never understand was the change in order that took place every week, from right to left. It then happened that the right-hand regiments, which had gotten their ration at 8:30 in the morning, received their next ration the next day at nine o'clock at night, thirty-six hours later.

It is easy to understand the physical hardships that the men went through. One night I observed the distribution that my regiment had awaited for thirty-six hours. When the bell rang to announce the arrival of the wagon, the starving men ran towards it. A freezing rain had fallen since the day before, spoiling the road and further delaying the wagon's arrival. When it finally stopped at the spot where the distribution was to take place, its armed guards had all the pains in the world to stop the prisoners from attacking it. The hungriest were literally howling, and later I saw these poor men, still hungry, rush to the barrels to scrape them with their bare hands and swallow the last morsels. This took place in a corner of camp lit only by a few smoky torches, and was such an indescribably sinister scene that I will never forget it. Such deprivation, added to the suffering already endured in Metz and the exhaustion of fighting, could only make for more casualties among the prisoners. For many, barely escaped from the massacres of Gravelotte, Saint-Privat, and Servigny, the Prussians could have described this new hell by writing on the front gate, "Abandon all hope, you who enter here!"

The Suffering of the Prisoners

WHEN THE PRISONERS managed to receive a bit of money, some time later, they were able to greatly improve their pitiful lot. In addition, many used their ingenuity to find jobs. Tailors in particular had plenty to do, because those prisoners who had managed to keep their blankets had them made over into coats that helped to keep out the bitter cold better than their ragged tunics did.

Those who had passes to work in town, as well as the officers' orderlies, could come and go as they pleased. They were only held to appear at roll call at fixed hours two or three times a week, and to respect a seven-o'clock curfew in the evening. Any worker or orderly found outside camp after curfew was brought back and risked not only a sanction but the removal of his pass.

Some prisoners set up a black-market system, obtaining alcohol outside of camp and then selling it under the name "Morning Drop." Gambling games were common in some parts of camp, where one could risk a few coins playing "Red or Black." Sometimes coffee or stews were made with potatoes stolen by prisoners on kitchen duty by resorting to ruses that only a trooper could dream up.

For instance, having made a coat with the sleeves sewn shut, prisoners would fill up the arms with potatoes. It was relatively easy then, under cover of darkness, to sling the coat over one's shoulder and walk away with the stolen food. Becoming more ingenious with time, prisoners invented other ways of stealing, until at one time we actually had a stock of three hundred kilos of potatoes. Unfortunately, one day news of this leaked out, and from then on all men on kitchen duty were searched. It was the end of the potato thieves, but in time the soldiers found other means of exercising their ingenuity.

* * *

I have heard that prisoners interned in other parts of Germany say the bugles that brought them to roll call were French, and so were the buglers, but I can affirm that in the Mainz prison camp the bugler was definitely German, using a raucous horn that sounded less than military.

According to international regulations, prisoners of war were to spend a regular amount of time in work or exercises meant to help them keep fit and boost morale. During our stay in Mainz, we were mainly employed unloading planks of wood from boats on the Rhine river, which we loaded onto wagons and then dragged back to camp ourselves. The hill leading to camp was so steep that it was not unusual to see forty to fifty men yoked to each wagon to pull it.

These planks were meant to build barracks destined to replace the tents in which we slept, eighteen to twenty men apiece, until November 20. We were assigned to help the German construction workers build these barracks. As there was little water in the prison camp, we had to obtain it from a village 600 meters away. The "Morning Drop" traffickers mentioned previously made sure to be part of the detail ordered to go there, to use the opportunity to renew our supply of alcohol.

There was also another water pump we could go to on the trail leading from town to the prison camp, and every day, morning and night, four men were detached there to set it up. Sometimes they spent half an hour just unthawing it before they could get at the water.

One day I was ordered on this detail with two of my roommates. One of them, named Lecoq, from Auch, was an intelligent young man that I very much liked. On our way he told me the story of how pure luck had saved him from the firing squad.

At the beginning of the war he had signed up with a company of sharpshooters. One day, ambushed and surrounded by Prussians, they had had to barricade themselves in a farm. When their ammunitions were gone, seeing that there was no chance of escape, they were forced to surrender, knowing full well that they would not be spared. There were twenty of these devilishly brave men, commanded by their captain, who ordered them to line up in two rows outside with their weapons on the ground in front of them. The Prussians immediately took the weapons and prepared for a mass execution. At this moment a German general chanced to arrive on the scene; he suddenly recognized the captain, with whom he had been friends before the war in Biarritz. He intervened on their behalf and was able to obtain a promise from the Prussian commander that the entire company be spared and sent into captivity.

As we told each other our various miseries, the two-hour duty passed. Returning to camp at eleven, we were surprised to find that all the prisoners had been forced to line up for inspection. When I asked the reason for this unusual order, I found out that a visit was expected from Princess Frederic-Charles. Our august visitor did not worry too much about the men, as she showed up only at half past one.

German lieutenants were revoltingly brutal, even towards their own soldiers. But if these soldiers accepted brutality, it was their own choice, whereas we prisoners had to accept everything without protest. One day I saw a sapper who was in the terminal stages of tuberculosis and could hardly stand up. He arrived a little late at roll call. The lieutenant in charge attacked him with such violence that the poor man fell down, never to rise again, opening his eyes just once to reproach the lout for having so despicably abused his power.

I mentioned before that our prison camp was located on the heights of Mainz. On the other side, on a hill across a ravine, was the cemetery. Every morning the musket volleys accompanying the corpses to be buried would enable us to count how many of us would never see our native land again.

The camp was placed between the fort and the ramparts. Cannons had been placed on either side so that we would have been immediately shot had we tried to escape. These precautions had been taken after rumors had circulated that Garibaldi was planning to come deliver the prisoners, give them arms, and take over the German stronghold with their help. We were very much aware of these rumors, without knowing for sure to what degree they were true, but the idea was a good one and might well have worked.

One day when I returned from pump duty I had a wonderful surprise. I had two visitors, Mr. Yung and Mr. Traut, directors of the Kursaal* of Wiesbaden, to whom I had written some time before. They had a valid authorization to take me to work for them. Although at the time they had no real need for a cook, as Alsatians and Frenchmen they looked for and seized upon every chance they could get to do something for the French prisoners. I am greatly indebted to these two generous and patriotic men, and I have never failed to let them know of my profound gratitude.

---

* The Kursaal was an elegant, colonnaded restaurant at Wiesbaden, the fashionable resort just outside Mainz. [ed.]

A Sinister Bonfire

FRENCH CHEFS BEFORE 1870 were well acquainted with Wiesbaden, a relatively posh resort at the time. The Kursaal was an impressive establishment and very well situated. It was not unpleasant to spend the summer months there. It had a big park, in the middle of which was a pond that served as a skating rink in the winter. When I got there, the kitchens were directed by Mr. Desjardins, a Frenchman who had been exempted from military service due to his age. His *rôtisseur* was a similarly exempted elderly man called Pierre. The latter came back to France with me in March and died after having held several jobs as chef, including at the Restaurant Grosse-Tête. There was also a sauce chef called Richard whom I later saw in London, and Léger, a young eighteen-year-old who left us to sign up in the army in the North and later received a facial wound. By a curious coincidence I would meet up again with Léger after the insurrection of the Commune, as he would be with me for the reopening of Le Petit Moulin Rouge.

I had been in Wiesbaden barely ten days when MacMahon arrived with his chiefs of staff. The Maréchal, with all of his family and his personal *chef de cuisine*, Jules Servi, moved into a house on the Sonnenbergstrasse ("Sun Mountain" street). Mr. Traut was asked to find a *chef de cuisine* for the chiefs of staff; he recommended me, and I was accepted. Due to this circumstance I can say that during the war of 1870 I worked as the chef of the two major Army General Headquarters.

A little later General de Gallifet arrived with the Count of Beaumont, the Maréchal's brother-in-law, and they asked the Kursaal to recommend a cook. I immediately proposed Bouniol, who was beginning to go gray making his spice cakes, and I arranged for him to come. It was a great joy to be together again, far from the cursing of the German lieutenants and from that miserable camp where so many of our friends still fretted away their time.

The chiefs of staff I served were housed in a villa located about a hundred meters away from MacMahon's house, on the same street but on the other side. This street started at the Kursaal and ran through the Sonnenbergstrasse to a high point on the outskirts of town. From here I once watched a sight not mentioned by any historian that I know of.

* * *

As soon as the preliminary conditions of the Peace Treaty became known in Germany, the whole country experienced a great sense of relief because, in spite of the persistently encouraging war reports, the German people feared a sudden change of fortune. The memory of Napoléon I remained fixed in every German heart, and up until the very last moment they nursed a haunting fear that only the news of a decisive victory could banish. When they finally heard the news of the Peace Treaty, the Germans could think of no fitting way to express their overwhelming joy. Their pride had never been so vocal. They had actually conquered a descendant of the Great French Emperor, and this victory, which they had still not been sure of just the day before, completely intoxicated them.

They resolved to build a tremendous bonfire to celebrate the event, and the town council issued an appeal to the population of Wiesbaden to donate their old wood. A huge woodpile was rapidly built up, and on that evening, at about eight o'clock, all the inhabitants of Wiesbaden crowded into the Sonnenbergstrasse to have the best view of the magnificent spectacle about to unfold.

The ever-growing crowd had their eyes fixed on the woodpile, waiting for the purifying flames to leap forth, but all they could see was a few men with torches trying desperately to light the fire. By who knows what miracle, or what misfortune, not a spark of fire rose from the dense clouds of smoke coming from the woodpile. Gasoline was poured onto the stubborn logs, and the smoke only became darker and more intense. There was general disappointment, and the crowd dispersed slowly.

There was, however, a perfectly natural explanation. The inhabitants of Wiesbaden, called upon to donate wood for the bonfire, had taken good care not to sacrifice their best-burning logs. Each man had convinced himself that in such a furnace, everything would burn like straw. The result was that the pile was composed exclusively of old, damp wood which had lain so long in the cellars that it had become practically unburnable.

The coincidence still must have had a supernatural element, for chance alone would not have brought about such a result. I stayed at my observation post for a long time with my friends surrounding me, feeling a truly immense relief after the trials of the past months.

End of the War and Back to Home

At the villa chosen for General Headquarters, the kitchens were well established and provisions were abundant in quantity and variety. I could have delved into *haute cuisine*, but given the situation, my chiefs of staff decided to keep to very simple family menus.

Lunch therefore consisted of:

Eggs or Fish
• • •
Meat
• • •
Vegetables
• • •
Sweet or Dessert
• • •
Coffee

Dinner was:

Soup

• • •

Some Kind of Fish

• • •

Roast Beef or Mutton

• • •

Salad

• • •

Vegetables

• • •

Sweet or Dessert

• • •

Coffee

When I didn't serve fish to begin with, I served roast fowl or game, and then the main dish. Venison, hares, partridges, woodcocks, and hazel grouse were all to be found in abundance, and if my officer's decision had not be so firm, I could easily have extended and varied my menus.

I must say that our stay in Wiesbaden would not have been at all disagreeable if it hadn't been for the sad circumstances bringing us there. Just as in Mainz, even if the inhabitants did not have exaggerated feelings of sympathy for us, they still found many ways to make us feel that we were not complete intruders. During my stay in Wiesbaden I never heard a single derogatory comment about us, and even the soldiers were extremely correct in their behavior towards us. Of course, it is obvious that if the German lieutenants had in any way shown themselves to be as brutal as their comrades in Mainz, our officers would have immediately taken action in defense of their soldiers.

Among the many visions of the disastrous war of 1870 that I have kept, there is one that I always think about at Christmastime. During that terrible year, Christmas was a horrible season; bloody fighting was still taking place at the gates of Paris and the thousands of French prisoners interned in all the prison camps of Germany were in pain, thinking of the parents, friends, and especially fiancées they had left at home and whom they might never see again.

But let me return to these memories that I wanted to evoke from so long ago. In that year of 1870, on Christmas Eve, I had been in Wiesbaden for several weeks, working as *chef de cuisine* for the chiefs of staff of MacMahon, and my situation was a very good one compared to that of the other prisoners of war that I had left behind in the prison camp at Mainz. I thought about them all the time, and especially of my friends whom I knew still had to survive on a simple bowl of lentils, haricot beans, or potatoes, with maybe a small slice of beef or pork fat.

Suddenly the idea came to me that I could spend the night of Christmas with them, and maybe bring them some decent food. It was easy for me to get a pass to go to the prison camp. I got to Mainz at around 5:30 in the evening, carrying some victuals and a few bottles of strong wine that was of good quality, even if it was neither Burgundy nor Champagne.

As far as I can remember there are only a few kilometers from Wiesbaden to Mainz. During the trip there, I did think that my unexpected appearance would make my friends happy. But I never forgot the wild enthusiasm with which they greeted me. They were delirious. And they all asked me of news from their families, as if they thought I had come directly from each of their own villages.

It took them a while to think of the food I had brought. The table was quickly set. There were no tables or chairs, obviously, so we put all the food on a camp bed and everyone squatted around it. A candle stuck at the head of the bed lent light to our little scene, and no dinner had ever been so excellent.

This modest repast, which we would have otherwise taken with a great deal of joy and laughter, was still filled with sadness. It could not have been otherwise, in view of the deep, gaping wound that had been inflicted on our country. We all felt the same, and rose to lift our glasses and toast to the health of our families and our friends who, in the face of the enemy, continued to defend the honor of France. We also drank to the honor of the prisoners that destiny had sent to an enemy land. And while we had our miserable little celebration, other, more miserable men ran with torches under a freezing rain to the call of a horn to obtain the miserable soup that they had waited for since the night before.

These are sad memories, visions that a man can never forget.

It was only 9:30 when I had to leave my unhappy friends, and I regretted it, because somehow I thought it would have been my duty to spend the entire bittersweet Christmas night with them.

*   *   *

On March 14, 1871, after the signing of the preliminary Peace Treaty, the French officers interned at Wiesbaden were free to return to France, as was the police force. Soldiers of the regular army had to await further decisions. As I belonged to the latter group, General de Gallifet requested special permission for me to leave, and I was given a pass for Paris at my own cost, which was not a problem for me.

As soon as I had my pass, I went to the station to buy my ticket for Metz, much more joyful than four months before when I had bought it in the other direction, for this time I was headed toward France and freedom, and I felt I had finally been returned to the unlimited horizons that I had before me. Pierre, the *rôtisseur* of the Kursaal, came with me.

After seeing the Beaubourg family and several friends in town, Pierre and I left by train to Paris. The train in question went only as far as Epernay, where we arrived at midnight. The train station was completely disorganized, to the extent that German soldiers had to accompany baggage transport to hotels. I did not have to worry about this, as I had little baggage. But Pierre had more, and as it was necessary to keep everything safe, a German soldier accompanied us to the inn where we were staying.

We spent the night there, after a good meal that was much needed, and the next day, at first light, we took the train to Pantin, which was the end of the line for the time being. It was obvious that these trains, driven by Prussians, could hardly enter into Paris.

The coachmen who proposed the next solution for bringing travelers from Pantin to Paris took advantage of it by asking exhorbitant prices. One of them that I asked did not hesitate to demand forty francs for the short trip. As we could not afford that kind of expense, we decided to go on foot. As far as I was concerned, considering what I had gone through during the war, this kind of trip did not faze me in the least, and my desire to see Paris again was far greater than any fear of being tired. Pierre therefore took care of the transport of his baggage for five francs, and we set off despite the awful weather. On that day, March 16, 1871, snow was falling on and off, and a glacial wind froze our faces.

When we got to the Pont-de-Flandre, we saw behind us several coachmen returning from Pantin without any passengers, obviously, and among them was the delightful gentleman who had asked us for forty francs to take us to Paris. We took our vengeance. Without speaking a word, we got into the coach and, once installed, asked him to take us to the Champs-Elysées. Then we generously paid him just exactly the proper fare for the trip.

When we got there, I said good-bye to Pierre and went home. Without eating, and having just cleaned myself up a bit, I went back down to find all the old friends that I had so much looked forward to seeing again. Everywhere one saw the traces of war and there was a feeling of depression and sadness. However, one felt that the Parisians wanted to get on with the life they had been accustomed to and finally forget the terrible nightmare. No such luck!

On March 18, the affair of the Montmartre cannons once again put Paris in upheaval. During the siege, public funds had been used to have these Montmartre cannons melted down, and they had been brought from Cours-la-Reine to Buttes-Montmartre by the regiments of the National Guard. Realizing the danger in leaving this artillery (about two hundred cannons or heavy machine guns) in the hands of the National Guard, the Government gave the formal order to get them back the next day at dawn.

A regiment of the Garde de Paris, commanded by artillery officers of the Pépinière barracks, was charged with this mission, which it could hardly carry out due to the lack of teams and wagons needed to remove the artillery. One of my friends, Bouillane de Saint-Martin, was part of this regiment, and he was arrested by federate soldiers with the others. Some were shot, and most were forgotten in prison until the regular army entered Paris. Some of them went crazy waiting. My friend Saint-Martin got married at the end of the Commune period, and then soon died. He left a son and a daughter that I took under my wing in his memory. Of his son, I made a cook.

This terrible day, when the regular army was seen making pacts with rioters (among them the Third *Bataillon de Chasseurs* and the Eighty-eighth *Bataillon de Marche*) and assassinating two generals, heralded the first beginnings of the movement that preceded the Commune. This meant that the prisoners of war arriving home from Germany had to fight once again, this time not against an outside enemy but against their fellow Frenchmen who disrupted order and organized the incredible insurrection that terrorized Paris for two months, and whose final curtain was at the Père Lachaise cemetery.

Bouniol, being detained by his duties, had not been able to leave when I did, but he soon came to join me. Together we followed the first events of the Commune.

On April 6, huge posters from the Central Committee were plastered on walls all over the city. They announced that all able-bodied men between the ages of eighteen and forty must take up arms for the Commune. As my personal opinions did not allow me to join the insurrection, and my situation, on the contrary, called for me to join the regular army as soon as possible, I decided to leave Paris at once. As it was, I was barely in time, as measures were soon taken to prevent all departures except for foreigners with passports. Without waiting, I rushed to the Gare Saint-Lazare, which I found to be occupied. I then went to the Gare du Nord, where I was lucky enough to catch the very last train that left Paris freely. After a great detour, I managed to get to MacMahon's General Headquarters at Versailles and find work in the kitchens under Jules Servi, and there I awaited the end of the actions taken against the Commune.

*   *   *

After Paris was taken by the troops of Versailles, General Headquarters was transferred to the Ministry of Foreign Affairs, along with MacMahon's entire family, in whose service I remained until August 14. It was during this time that, during a few days' leave, I helped with the reopening of Le Petit Moulin Rouge.

On August 15, I was assigned to the provisional Seventeenth Regiment occupying the neighborhoods of La Banque and Le Louvre. This regiment was under the command of Colonel Count de Waldner, who later became a general, and who soon hired me as *chef de cuisine*.

In the following spring, the regiment left Paris for the camp of Villeneuve l'Etang. The Colonel settled down in Ville d'Avray, next to Porte-Blanche. There, in the countryside, I had the leisure to discover the art of creating wax flowers.* I stayed there fourteen months, appreciating the esteem and friendship that the Colonel and his family had for me. This was a special time in my life, for the Count and Countess de Waldner were very interested in my work and encouraged me greatly. But the quiet life could not be mine forever. I needed a greater field in which to exercise my creativity, and I spoke to the Colonel about it. In September he let me have a six-month leave.

* Escoffier's first published work was entitled *Traité sur l'Art de Travailler les Fleurs en Cire* (1885) where he discusses the creation of inedible wax flowers for the decoration of culinary dishes. [ed.]

Part Four

An Era of Celebrities

Paris — Monte Carlo — Lucerne
1872 – 1889

Return to Le Petit Moulin Rouge

AFTER THE WAR, I returned home and started work as *chef de cuisine* at the Hôtel de Luxembourg in Nice with my devoted friend Bouniol. After the 1872–1873 winter season I left the Hôtel de Luxembourg and Nice and went to Paris, where I once again started to work for Le Petit Moulin Rouge, but this time as *chef de cuisine*.

During the years I spent at this famous restaurant, from 1873 to 1878, it was my honor to serve princes, dukes, the most important social and political figures, and the greatest of kings and powerful bankers, all of which gave me the opportunity to invent new gastronomic delights and train many new chefs.

Among the dishes I created at that time I should mention a few: *mousseline d'éperlans à la Pompadour, queues de petites langoustes à l'indienne, les cailles Lavallière, les suprêmes de poulets George Sand, le petit poulet de printemps Elisabeth la belle bouquetière, les coeurs d'artichauts Giralda, les suprêmes*

Prince Galitzin of Russia asked Escoffier to transform one of Le Petit Moulin Rouge's dining rooms into a "bower of roses" in honor of Blanche d'Antigny, an actress and successful demimondaine in Paris, St. Petersburg, and Bucharest. Escoffier completed the evening by creating a "rosy" dinner. The coupe d'Antigny created for the occasion was a strawberry sherbet swathed in a pinkish cloud of spun sugar.

d'écrevisses à la Vauclusienne, la timbale aux béatilles de Monseigneur, les soufflés Montmorency, and *la coupe d'Antigny,* dedicated to the beautiful Blanche d'Antigny, which was served for the first time during a dinner that Prince Galitzin gave in honor of this fine actress.

A small room for six had been reserved on this occasion, and the salon had been beautifully decorated with roses. Here is the menu I served:

Caviar Frais
Blinis
• • •
Consommé Rossolnick
Bouchées Moscovites
• • •
Mousselines d'Éperlans aux Crevettes Roses
• • •
Selle d'Agneau de Behague Poêlée
Petits Pois à la Française
Pommes Noisettes
• • •
Canetons de Rouen à la Rouennaise accompagnés d'une Fine Gelée au Frontignan
et de Coeurs de Romaines à l'Orange
• • •
Asperges d'Argenteuil
au Beurre Fondu
• • •
Soufflé au Fromage Périgourdine
• • •
Coupe d'Antigny
Gaufrettes Bretonnes
• • •
Café Mode Turque
Fine Vieille Champagne
Grande Chartreuse
• • •
Vins: Steinberger
Ausleye 1859
Mouton Rothschild
Mise au Château
• • •
Champagne (Servi Frais)
Veuve Clicquot, Goût Français

I met Prince Galitzin many years later at the Carlton Hotel in London, and he reminded me of the wonderful dinners of Le Petit Moulin Rouge. "I was young then," he told me, "and I was happy living the gay life. Of those wonderful days, I especially remember the times I spent in the company of charming young ladies. I often think back on those times, and it is my great regret not to be able to live them all over again."

In 1874 I met Sarah Bernhardt. The young actress had a role in a play where she was meant to be a sculptress, and knowing nothing of this art, she went to see the famous French painter Gustave Doré, who at that time was also a sculptor. His best creations in sculpture are a bronze vase called *La Vigne,* which recieved great acclaim at the 1882 Salon, and the lively and picturesque sculptures he created for the pedestal of the monument of Alexander Dumas that can be found on the Place Malesherbes.

In 1874 Sarah Bernhardt was attaining her full stature at the Comédie Française.

Gustave Doré warmly welcomed the future star and was happy to give her a few lessons. His studio at 5 rue Bayard was next door to Le Petit Moulin Rouge, and every time Sarah came for a lesson, the professor ordered a light meal to be sent from the restaurant for her. The meals were simple but carefully prepared. I was acquainted with Gustave Doré, as he usually came to the restaurant for lunch, and we often had the occasion to talk to each other. I knew his tastes and took great pleasure in preparing these light meals. I also knew of Sarah Bernhardt's passion for calf sweetbreads with fresh noodles served with a purée of *foie gras* and truffles. I often prepared it myself to make sure it was perfect for her. I think it is thanks to this dish that I owe the friendship and affection that she had for me. I often saw her later in Paris, London, New York, Aix-les-Bains, Lucerne, Nice, and for the last time in Monte Carlo, just before she died.

Gustave Doré (1832–1883), French illustrator, engraver, painter, and sculptor is best known for his highly imaginative and dramatic illustrations. His lively illustrations for some 120 books, including Paradise Lost, The Divine Comedy (1861), Don Quixote (1862), The Bible (1866), and other classics, are still admired.

I have the most respectful and affectionate memories of this brilliant actress. Sarah Bernhardt had a heart of gold. Here is a story that demonstrates her wonderful character. It dates from my recollections of England in 1906.

A French teacher called Bizeray had started a language school for young ladies in London. Classes were held every evening from seven to nine o'clock. The girls in these classes had heard so much of Sarah Bernhardt that they dreamed only of seeing her, speaking to her, maybe touching her dress. But how to get near to a goddess?

I was good friends with Bizeray, and he asked me to speak to Miss Bernhardt on behalf of his students. I did so, and when I explained my purpose, she started to laugh, but her laughter was so affectionate that I was sure she would do as I asked.

"Tell Bizeray that I will come and meet his students tomorrow night at eight o'clock." she said. And the next night I accompanied Miss Bernhardt on a surprise visit to these young ladies, a joyful visit that I am sure they have never forgotten.

* * *

When people want to meet each other outside of their homes, you can be sure that everything starts and ends with a meal!

One afternoon in July 1874, the Ministry sent me an usher with a card from Gambetta, requesting that a private salon be reserved for him at Le Petit Moulin Rouge, and ordering a meal including a saddle of Béhague lamb and a chicken en gelée with tarragon. He indicated that he would choose the wines upon arrival.

Remembering this meal, I realize that the famous *entente cordiale* between France and England that became official in 1907 was actually conceived many years earlier. In fact, on that evening, Gambetta's two guests were the Prince of Wales, the future King Edward VII, and another important foreign diplomat.

The Prince of Wales loved the Parisian lifestyle and French cuisine. Gambetta invited him several times to dinner at Le Petit Moulin Rouge. Everyone knew of their friendship and mutual understanding on many topics. These meals had a serious *raison d'être*, and it is probably in a room at Le Petit Moulin Rouge that the basic lines of the future entente cordiale were laid out. The menu I proposed to Gambetta in honor of the Prince of Wales in 1874 was the following one:

Melon Cantaloup
Porto Blanc
• • •
Consommé Royal
Paillettes Diablées
• • •
Filets de Sole aux Laitances à la Meunière
• • •
Selle d'Agneau de Béhague Poêlée
Haricots Verts à l'Anglaise
Pommes Noisettes à la Crème
• • •
Poularde en Gelée à l'Estragon
Salade d'Asperges
• • •
Soufflé d'Ecrevisses Rothschild
• • •
Biscuit Glacé Tortoni
Gaufrettes Normandes
• • •
Les Plus Belles Pêches de Montreuil
Amandes Vertes
• • •
Café Moka à la Française
Grande Fine Champagne
Liqueur des Chartreux
• • •
Vins Choisis: Chablis
Col d'Estounel, Etampé 1864
Veuve Clicquot, 1864

From Cannes to Paris

In 1876 I BOUGHT a food store in Cannes, Le Faisan Doré, and added on a restaurant room that would be open for the winter season.

On August 15, 1878, I left Le Petit Moulin Rouge for the last time, and on August 28 I married Delphine Daffis, the eldest daughter of Paul Daffis, a well-known editor and owner of the Elzevirienne Collection. Our marriage would give us two sons and a daughter: Paul, Daniel, and Germaine.

In early September, we returned to Cannes for the opening of Le Faisan Doré. We had been married barely two months when my father-in-law died suddenly, leaving a widow and two young daughters, the elder of whom was only three years old. Four months after their father's death, his two little daughters died, one after the other, both taken away within one week by whooping cough.

Because of these tragic events, I had to give up my business in Cannes. I needed to work, so I took the first opportunity that presented itself to me. By a stroke of luck, I had already met one of the owners of La Maison

Chevet, located near the Palais Royal in Paris, a business that had world-wide renown for catered meals and fine food. They needed a general manager. I was recommended for the job, and accepted it. I started right away and had to learn how the business was run as quickly as possible. Due to various circumstances, I stayed there as general manager for only eight months.

La Maison Chevet had built up a well-deserved reputation for catering fine meals for government ministries and wealthy bourgeois families in the provinces and even abroad in Germany, England, etc. Planning a meal to send to England was a delicate task, as one had to take into account the toll that a possible rough crossing of the Channel would take.

I have kept many good memories of the time I spent with La Maison Chevet. One of them was a village festival organized by Mrs. Adam (Juliette Lambert)* in her property in Gif. During the floods that devastated Alsace, Mrs. Adam had the generous idea of organizing an auction to help the victims of the disaster. She called for artists to donate their works to the auction, and 150 artists agreed. The sale of their valuable works raised a large sum of money that was turned over to the committee for the victims.

To thank the generous donors to this fund-raising project, Mrs. Adam organized a great celebration. The program consisted of a parade in the morning, headed by Mrs. Adam herself dressed up as a shepherdess; the parade was followed by lunch at picnic tables placed under the age-old trees in her property, and in the evening another meal was served by candlelight in the garden. An orchestra played to accompany some of the greatest tenors of the Opera.

Mrs. Adam spent her winters in Cannes and had been a regular client of Le Faisan Doré. I had often had the occasion to talk with her, and this is why she gave me the responsibility of organizing her luncheon, her dinner, and all the service required, which I did with great pleasure and devotion.

I left La Maison Chevet the next spring with warm memories of the time I had spent there, and stayed on very good terms with Mr. Chevet.

Shortly thereafter, in early May 1880, Messrs. Pellé and Adolphe, own-

La Maison Chevet was a famous catering firm whose premises in the Palais Royal had been a landmark for gourmets ever since the First Empire. Chevet's catered for embassies, princely houses, and government ministries, even dispatching dinners and banquets abroad to Germany or England, complete with cutlery, tableware, and waiters.

* French political writer. [ed.]

73

ers of the Restaurant de l'Opéra in Paris, hired me as *chef de cuisine* to open a new restaurant annexed to the casino in Boulogne-sur-Mer. The casino was a veritable palace, where orchestras, ballrooms, theaters, and all kinds of gambling games abounded for the pleasure of the summer clientèle.

The Café-Restaurant du Casino was one of the best restaurants in the area. Summer visitors were delighted to discover that it was on par with the finest restaurants in Paris. The service was so perfect, the cuisine so fine and delicate, the wine so exquisite, that customers might have imagined that they were in Paris on the boulevard Haussmann, if they had not had before their eyes a beautiful view of the beach and the sea extending all the way to the coast of England.

When the restaurant was first opened, Mr. Hirschler, one of the directors of the Boulogne-sur-Mer resort, organized a splendid three-day celebration. It included a succession of shows and productions with some of the finest artists brought in from Paris. One of the most appreciated shows was a ballet in the style of Les Folies Bergères, during which a dance by eight seductive French women disguised as shrimp fisherwomen was especially applauded.

The inaugural banquet was served in the new restaurant room. I found myself at the press table, where the journalists seemed to be more preoccupied with tasting the succession of dishes and fine wines that were being served than with the inaugural speeches that were being made; they seemed to recognize the great importance of tasting a new wine, and the speeches could have been in French or in Chinese, as far as they were concerned!

At the end of the summer season I returned to Paris and immediately found work at the Restaurant Maire with Mr. Paillard.[*] At that time the Restaurant Maire had an excellent reputation for its fine cuisine and magnificent wine cellar. Its clients certainly kept fond memories of the meals we concocted, such as *canard au sang*, *bécasse flambée*, *perdreaux en cocotte parfumés de mousserons frais et de truffes*, not to mention a divine *langouste à la crème* and an unforgettable *pomme marie*.

---

[*] Famous nineteenth-century Parisian restaurateur whose establishment was frequented by all the Parisian elite. The duck "au sang" was highly reputed. [ed.]

Monte Carlo and Lucerne
My Meeting with César Ritz,
and Other Memories

I N OCTOBER 1884, I left Mr. Paillard to return to Monte Carlo and become restaurant manager of the Grand Hôtel, belonging to Mrs. Jungbluth. It was at the Grand Hôtel of Monte Carlo that I met César Ritz. The name of Ritz has since earned world-wide renown.

When we first met in Monte Carlo, Ritz was looking for someone to help him extend his expertise in the hotel management industry. He himself was not a cook, and he needed a chef who knew all the secrets of the art of *haute cuisine*, who knew everything about restaurant service and the intricacies of *à la carte* dining. He asked me to work for him, and the ideas and thoughts that we both believed in helped us to work together in total harmony and understanding. From that day until his death during World War I, in fact, we were inseparable friends.

After the winter season in Monte Carlo, Ritz would manage the Hôtel National in Lucerne in the summer. The next year I went to work with him

The Jungbluth family had recently bought the Grand Hôtel in Monte Carlo and appointed Ritz as manager. Its competition was the newly built and luxurious Hôtel de Paris, owned by the same group that owned the casino. When Ritz lost his chef, Giroix, to its rival, the latter proposed Escoffier to replace him. In those days, restaurant service in hotels, even in luxury establishments, was still table d'hôte, or a practice of one seating, usually at a long central table, at a set hour when all guests ate together. The idea of luxury restaurants providing à la carte service was therefore a novelty.

there and later, in 1890, we were in complete agreement when he decided to take on the management of the Savoy Hotel in London, and that I would direct the kitchens of this new hotel.

At that time the restaurant of the Grand Hôtel in Monte Carlo was the meetingplace of high society. The most important people dined there, coming from all over the world: England, America, France, Germany, Austria, Russia, Italy, etc. The Grand Duke of Mecklemburg, who spent his winters in Cannes, came to Monte Carlo once a week to lunch at the Grand Hôtel with his entourage, where a table was regularly reserved for him.

Many other influential people frequented the restaurant, such as Chamberlain, Lord Derby, Herbert Bismarck, and the Grand Dukes of Russia. The Prince of Wales, future King Edward VII, was a regular client. Here is a menu that I once served him:

....

Caviar Frais
Blinis au Sarrazin
• • •
Velouté d'Ecrevisse au Beurre d'Isigny
• • •
Nostèles à l'Anglaise
• • •
Selle d'Agneau de Lait de Pauillac
Petits Pois Frais du Pays
Pommes de Terre Rosette
• • •
Perdreaux Cocotte Périgourdine
Salade de Laitues Rouges
• • •
Coeurs d'Artichauts à la Moëlle et Parmesan
• • •
Mousse à la Vanille accompagnée de Cerises Jubilée[*]
• • •
Friandise de Monte-Carlo
• • •
Café Mode Turque

[*] *Les cerises jubilée,* cherries jubilee, was a dessert created in honor of the fiftieth anniversary of the reign of Her Royal Majesty Queen Victoria, Queen of England and Empress of India. [ed.]

Grande Fine Champagne 1860
Chartreuse du Couvent

• • •

Champagne Brut Lafite, 1874
Porto Vieux

* * *

Some of my friends, visiting Monte Carlo in 1887, were strongly tempted by the casino's gambling tables. After spending a few hours gambling, they were delighted with their winnings and decided to convert them into a fine meal. They reserved a table at the Grand Hôtel at the last minute, and we prepared the following meal, accompanied by the finest wines:

Prélude
Frivolités de la Riviera
Oeufs de Pluviers au Poivre Oriental
Caviar de Sterlet
Crêpes Mousseline
Vodka

• • •

Timbale de Queues de Langoustines de la Méditerannée au Paprika Rose
Riz Pilaf
Jeune Agneau de Pâques Renaissance
Petits Pois Frais à l'Anglaise
Pommes Nouvelles Châtelaine

• • •

Suprême de Poulet en Gelée à l'Alsacienne
Salade d'Asperges aux Truffes

• • •

Coeurs d'Artichauts au Parmesan

• • •

Biscuit Glacé à l'Orange
Fraises au Curaçao
Gaufrettes aux Avelines

• • •

Café à la Française
Grande Fine Champagne
Vieille Chartreuse du Couvent

Recipe for Timbale de Langoustine au Paprika Rose
(SERVES 10)

Choose 6 prawns (about 300 grams) and divide them in half lengthwise. Remove the small pocket near the head, which often contains gravel. Set aside the creamy parts found next to this small pocket, remove the legs, and cut each prawn half into two pieces. Season with salt and pepper. In a saucepan, heat 100 grams of butter with a large spoonful of pure olive oil. Place the pieces of prawn side by side in the butter and cover the saucepan as soon as their shells start to brown. Add a spoonful of finely chopped onion and shallots, 250 grams of carefully chosen and peeled fresh mushrooms, and a dessert spoonful of red paprika. Cover the saucepan and let the onions and mushrooms simmer for a few minutes. Add a few teaspoons of aged Armagnac and a large glass of white wine. Continue simmering to reduce the sauce by half, and add 4 deciliters of fish *velouté* and 3 teaspoons of meat glaze. Cover the saucepan and continue simmering for 20 minutes. At this point, remove the pieces of prawn, peel them and place them in a silver timbale, keeping them warm. Add the reserved creamy parts, 100 grams of fresh butter, the juice of one lemon, and a little freshly chopped parsley. Thicken the sauce with 4 egg yolks beaten with fresh cream and complete it with the butter sauce. Immediately pour the sauce over the prawns and serve hot with a rice pilaf.

* * *

During the 1885–1886 season, Katinka,* the great Hungarian ballerina came to stay at the Grand Hôtel in Monte Carlo. Russian Prince Kochubey, who was also staying at the hotel, often invited her to dine with him.

I frequently had the occasion to talk to this wonderful dancer, and she enjoyed telling me of the food of her native country, which was of particular interest to me. Of these conversations I have kept a few recipes that I used several times, including the one for *foie gras* with paprika.

---

* Katinka, one of the most attractive and successful demimondaines, was a Hungarian ballerina, and had a keen appreciation for fine food and dishes from the homeland. [ed.]

We were talking of crayfish one day, and the dancer said to me, "I love crayfish, but I hate having to peel their shells off at the table. Could you serve them without their shells?" The next night, as she was dining with the Prince and two other influential members of the Russian community, I served them the following menu:

Caviar Gris de Sterlet
Blinis Moscovite
Vodka
• • •
Velouté Léger de Poulet
Paillettes aux Amandes Grillées
• • •
Mousse de Merlan aux Ecrevisses
(that I called *"Le Rêve de Katinka,"* Katinka's Dream)
• • •
Selle d'Agneau de Pauillac Poêlée
Petits Pois Frais à l'Anglaise
Pommes Rosette
• • •
Cailles à la Hongroise
(Quail poached in a brown veal sauce,
served cold in their glaze, with *foie gras*,
prepared according to Katinka's recipe)
• • •
Asperges de Serre au Beurre Fondu
• • •
Soufflé au Parmesan à la Périgourdine
• • •
Fraises au Curaçao
Fleurettes Chantilly
Sablés Viennois
• • •
Café Mode Orientale
Vieille Fine Champagne
Grande Chartreuse

Some may think that choosing whiting for the fish course was somewhat vulgar, but they would be wrong. Whiting has a bad reputation that it does not merit. Its flesh is excellent for the health, light, flaky, and not too moist, it is easily digestible and often recommended as an excellent dish for convalescents. If whiting had a fancy name like "starfish," it would be declared the king of fish.

Recipe for Mousse de Merlan aux Ecrevisses
(Le Rêve de Katinka)

(serves 5–6)

Buy very fresh whiting and remove the fillets (make sure to carefully take out all of the bones and nerves). For each 500 grams of fillet obtained, set aside 3 egg whites, 6–7 deciliters of thick fresh cream, 12 grams of salt, and 1 gram of fresh pepper. Add the seasoning to the flesh of the fish, crushing it and mixing well. Add the egg whites one at a time and pass the mixture through a fine sieve. Place the mixture in a well-silvered saucepan (called a *sauteuse*) and cool it on ice for 45 minutes. Then work the cream into the mousse with a wooden spoon, keeping the *sauteuse* on ice during the whole time.

Carefully butter a large charlotte mold, place a few slices of truffle in the bottom of the mold and around its sides, and fill it 3/4 of the way up with the mousse mixture. Cover the mold and poach it in a double boiler *au bain Marie,* making sure the water simmers but never boils.

While the mousse is cooking, boil 36 large shrimp in a white wine court bouillon. Remove their shells and place the tails in a saucepan with 2 teaspoons of butter and 125 grams of raw truffle, peeled and sliced, and a little salt and pepper. Cover the saucepan and heat the shrimp for several minutes, until the aroma of the truffles is perfect. Incorporate the paprika cream sauce. Just before serving, unmold the mousse onto a round platter and surround it with the shrimp sauce.

Mousse de merlan "Rêve de Katinka" must be as light and delicate as the airy steps of this famous dancer.

The next morning, this gracious Hungarian lady came into the kitchen to thank me for the excellent dinner they had been served. It had been the fulfillment of a gourmet's dream and her guests had also been delighted. The Prince was soon going to have other guests and it was his wish that the same menu be offered. "But," she told me confidentially, "I know that he loves that fine amphibian you call a frog, and as I know you always have beautiful ones, could you add a few frog's legs to the shrimp?" I did so, of course, and I don't have to tell you the success of that surprise.

Dinner with *"La Patti"*

THE GREAT DIVA Adelina Patti, who fully appreciated a warm welcome wherever she went, was one day invited to the Grand Hôtel by its owners, Mr. and Mrs. Jungbluth. She always enjoyed being able to come back there. Her immense talent had never gone to her head; she had become a friend to all of us, and she loved discussing cooking with Mr. Jungbluth.

One day, while Miss Patti was lunching at the restaurant, she asked Mr. Jungbluth the following question, with that pixie air of hers that was so much part of her charm. "Tell me," she said, "I've noticed that you are in perfect health, so I suppose you don't eat all this rich food all the time. Couldn't you serve me some of your own simple family meals?"

Mr. Jungbluth replied, "Nothing could be easier, and if you would do us the honor of lunching with my family tomorrow, we are having an excellent Alsatian *pot-au-feu* that I believe will certainly meet with your approval."

Miss Patti accepted the invitation with pleasure, and it was with her usual great simplicity that she came to lunch, accompanied by a lady friend.

The menu I conceived was an Alsatian *pot-au-feu* prepared with the following recipe.

In an earthenware pot, place a rump of beef and pieces of salt pork from Alsace. Cover the meat with cold salted water (7 grams of salt for one liter of water). Bring it to a boil, carefully skimming the scum off as it comes up. Add the necessary vegetables and simmer the mixture for 3 hours over a very small flame, keeping the pot partially uncovered.

I first served a *potage Xavier* made up of the excellent bouillon of the *pot-au-feu*. Then I served the rump of beef on a long platter, surrounded by all of its vegetables, sausage, and bacon, and accompanied by a horseradish sauce *mode alsacienne* that perfectly enhanced the taste of the dish.

I then served an excellent chicken *de la Bresse*, that I had barded with strips of lard and roasted on a open spit, and also a mixed salad of chicory leaves and beets.

In view of the occasion, I thought we would be forgiven for expanding this "simple family meal" and gave in to the small sin of gourmandise. Therefore a magnificent *parfait de foie gras* also appeared on the table. This *pâté*, which I baptized *Sainte-Alliance*, was made up of a mixture of Alsatian *foie gras* and Périgord truffles, a truly unforgettable union. Despite all the political events troubling the atmosphere, the *parfait Sainte-Alliance* will ever remain one of the treasures of French cuisine.

I completed this exceptional family meal with an orange mousse surrounded by strawberries macerated in Curaçao.

At the beginning of the meal I had served a delicious light wine, the Zwikerb, but for the *foie gras,* it was necessary to bring out a traditional and exquisite Riesling, a famous vintage from Wolscheim, Mr. Jungbluth's native birthplace, and with this wine we duly celebrated the baptism of the *parfait Sainte-Alliance.*

* * *

I could make a long list of the dishes I created during this period: *la timbale Grimaldi, les filets de sole Walewska, les filets de sole florentine, la mousse de merlan aux huîtres à l'orientale, poularde Monte-Carlo, poularde aux raviolis à la Garibaldi, le poulet sauté florentine, les suprêmes de perdreaux Marquise, les cailles Richelieu, les cailles Carmen, les cailles du Chevalier Lombard, la poularde Adelina Patti, les fraises Mireille, les mandarines surprise, la mousse de merlan Katinka, etc.*

All of these new dishes created in Monte Carlo had to be revised for the Hôtel National in Lucerne, as both hotels shared the same clientéle.

At that time, I spent the winter season at the Grand Hôtel in Monte Carlo and the summer season at the Hôtel National in Lucerne. In spite of its age, the latter was a beautiful palace that had been able to maintain its high prestige and world wide reputation, as it was constantly being improved and modernized in the best possible ways. The Hôtel National had been built on the shores of a beautiful lake, the Vierwaldstättersee, and had an ideal view, with the Righi on the left, the Pilatus on the right, the lake with its sailboats in front, and the beautiful snow-covered mountain range in the distance. On an early summer's morning it was possible to open the balcony doors of one's room and in perfect privacy, stretch out to the first rays of the sun and breathe in the fine air of the surrounding flower-filled mountains.

At the Hôtel National, guests were so well treated that they always looked forward to their next visit. An excellent cuisine, the best list of French wines, and perfect service made it so that clients never wanted to leave.

The concept of a recipe in Indian cuisine is unknown. Each cook worked his own way. This was difficult for Escoffier to understand and hence it was a challenge for him to learn la cuisine hindoue. *In the 1890s the Savoy employed an Indian-born cook to provide their patrons with authentic curries.*

Many famous people stayed at the Hôtel National in Lucerne when I was restaurant manager there. The Empress Eugénie stayed for a short visit and was delighted. Prince Fouad, who became King Fouad I of Egypt, spent two or three weeks there every year. The Indian Maharajah de Baroda, on a trip to Europe for the Jubilee of Queen Victoria, Empress of India, stayed at the hotel for a month, with the Maharani and a suite of forty-five people, including an Indian cook and several Indian women whose sole task in life was to prepare the dough for the day's curry. Upon their arrival a special kitchen was set aside for them, and at each meal the Maharajah was served Indian meals as well as French dishes, which the Indian prince very much appreciated. The princess especially liked small fish from the lake served fried in olive oil.

The Count of Fontalva, the Portuguese ambassador to Switzerland, who often liked to organize balls and festivities on the lake, arrived every year from Lisbon in a superb Mail Coach pulled by six mules. His Royal Highness Prince George of Prussia, cousin to Emperor Wilhelm I, often came with his officers.

When French President Thiers retired on May 24, 1873, he was advised, for medical reasons, to take a long holiday. Mr. Jungbluth, who was still director of the Hôtel National, jumped at the occasion to be of assistance to him, and asked him to do him the honor of coming to Lucerne. Mr. Thiers was touched by such an invitation on the part of a patriotic French Alsatian and confirmed his arrival in a very cordial letter. As the lakefront of the Vierwaldstättersee seemed to be the ideal spot for retirement, the former president moved into the hotel with his wife and sister-in-law, Miss Dosne.

During the stay of this great statesman, many representatives of Committees of Alsatian Veterans came to present him with the colors of their regiments, to express their great respect, and to declare their allegiance to France. Mr. Thiers received them all with his usual cordiality, shook hands with them, and had a kind word for everyone. These demonstrations showed the attachment that Alsatians have for France, their birthplace.

Escoffier was very patriotic as were most Frenchmen. Deep-seated resentment against the Germans would endure until after World War I and the Treaty of Versailles when France regained Alsace, Lorraine, and their honor.

Part Five

From the Savoy to the Ritz

London — Rome — Paris
1890–1898

The Savoy Hotel
A Thundering Success

THE SAVOY was a prestigious hotel and restaurant built in 1888. It opened in 1889 and its future seemed very promising, but the glamour soon faded. Three months after its brilliant opening, it was facing bankruptcy. This could not have been otherwise, as the direction of the hotel had been entrusted to a charming man who unfortunately had no knowledge of hotel administration and no contacts or relations with hotel managers abroad, which was a bad mistake.

The restaurant was managed by a chef who was probably an excellent cook, as he had worked for Rothschild, but who had very little notion of how to manage a large restaurant with *à la carte* menus. In January 1890, therefore, César Ritz was asked to become the director of the Savoy Hotel, and he said to me, "You must come help me in this matter, and take over the management of the restaurant."

I knew a few things about the situation of the hotel, and was sure that it could be a great success, so I agreed to follow Ritz to London. We start-

On August 6, 1889, Richard d'Oyly Carte opened the Savoy Hotel in London, an opulent palace equipped with the latest modern innovations, including electric lights throughout and bathrooms for 250 rooms. The Victoria Hotel, the top London hotel at that time, had only four bathrooms for 500 guests. The kitchens of the Savoy Hotel became known for their modern equipment, and the unusually large amount of daylight that filtered through. These conditions were considered luxurious for most chefs, especially those from France.

ed work on the first Sunday in April 1890, assisted by a mutual friend, L. Echenard, who had directed the Midland Hotel in London for several years. We all shared the same ideas about hotel management, and our perfect understanding gave us confidence that we would succeed. Indeed, the Savoy Hotel, including its restaurant, soon became a model of modern hotel management and greatly served to implant French cuisine in England.

I still haven't forgotten the disagreeable surprise of the first day of our arrival at the Savoy. It was on a Sunday, when all stores in England are closed and it is nearly impossible to buy anything. We discovered that our predecessors, for reasons of their own, had broken everything that could have been useful for us and ruined the supplies they had left. We couldn't even find a grain of salt. Faced with this unpleasant circumstance, I called upon a good friend, Louis Peyre, director of the kitchens of the Charring Cross Hotel, and with great kindness he put at my disposal everything that I needed to address the situation rapidly. Thanks to him we got through the day without too many problems.

By the next day, Monday, everything was back in working order, but it was time to move quickly with new ideas to be able to attract the attention of the elite in English society. We started our innovations immediately.

We had already noticed at the Grand Hôtel in Monte Carlo that our English clients, faced with *à la carte* menus written in French that they could not understand, often asked the *maître d'hôtel* to order the meal for them. This was the same case at the Savoy, where the menus were also written in French. Together, Ritz, Echenard, and I agreed to change this by creating a *prix fixe* menu that contained most of the items offered on the *à la carte* menu. There had to be a minimum of four people at the table to order a *prix fixe* meal, and I took care of composing the menus myself.

We immediately implemented this system, and here is how it worked. When a customer requested a *prix fixe* menu, the *maître d'hôtel* would take down his name in a notebook, including the number of people in the party and the hour of the reservation. He would immediately send me the order, and I would then invent a menu. I kept a carbon copy of the menu I had composed in a special book so that the next time the same person ordered a

Prix fixe meals first began at poor-quality and inexpensive eating establishments that offered meals to the industrial working class population. The most famous was perhaps the Bouillons Duval, established in 1855 and later becoming the Parisian chain, La Table d'Hôte. The 1862 edition of Paris Guide recommended these to readers who wanted inexpensive meals.

prix fixe meal, I could be sure not to serve him the same dishes twice. I had great freedom in the composition of these menus, which enabled me to vary them at will and thus produce many new creations. Our *prix fixe* menus became very popular and played a large part in the success of the Savoy. They still existed forty years after they were implemented.

I must say that because I loved to cook, I took special pleasure in composing these menus, both to please my customers and to satisfy my own pride.

Ritz had taken great care in the lighting of the restaurant, making sure there was a soft and flattering glow that would enhance the beauty of our lady customers. Very appreciative of this attention, our female clientèle grew rapidly and became very faithful patrons. Knowing how to enhance a woman's natural beauty is one of the secrets of success.

In Victorian London of the 1880s and 1890s actresses, singers, and demi-mondaines were the kinds of women seen in public places. Wives or English ladies were reluctant to dine in public restaurants for fear of being mistaken as mistresses.

Shortly thereafter, with some initial difficulty, we were able to get the authorization to have an orchestra play during dinner on Sunday nights, something that had never existed in England before. It was a great innovation that was so successful that every restaurant in London rushed in to copy the example.

The restaurant of the Savoy Hotel rapidly became the meeting place of London's elite. Every night the greatest members of English and foreign aristocracy could be found dining there along with the most influential bankers and famous celebrities in the world of art.

* * *

The marriage of Princess Hélène, the sister of Duke of Orléans, to Duke of Aosta, was held at the Savoy. On this occasion, thirty-seven princes and princesses, dukes and duchesses occupied a sumptuous table in one salon, while their entourages occupied another room nearby. On the very same day, the Cornish Club ordered a banquet for fifty of their members, to be presided over by the Prince of Wales. As the prince was obliged to attend the latter event, the Princess of Wales represented the royal family at the wedding reception next door. On that day I therefore had to serve three very prestigious tables, more than 150 people, for whom the following three separate menus had been prepared.

91

Menu for the Royal Wedding Reception of the Duke of Aosta to Princess Hélène, Sister of the Duke of Orléans

Table d'Honneur

Melon Cantaloup
Frontignan

• • •

Consommé en Gelée
Velouté de Champignons à l'Italienne

• • •

Truite Saumonée Pochée au Vin d'Asti
accompagnée de Paupiettes de Sole à la Montpensier

• • •

Selle de Mouton de Pré Salé à la Piémontaise
Petits Pois à la Française
Pommes Noisettes

• • •

Suprêmes de Volaille Royale Alliance
Pointes d'Asperges à la Crème

• • •

Sorbets au Clicquot Rosé

• • •

Cailles aux Feuilles de Vigne
Brochettes d'Ortolans
Salade Victoria

• • •

Coeurs d'Artichauts à la Moelle
Soufflé d'Ecrevisses à la Florentine

• • •

Pêches Princesse Louise d'Orléans
Dressées sur Mousse à la Fraise
Friandises

• • •

Les Plus Beaux Fruits
Café Mode Orientale
Fines Liqueurs de France

Guest Table

Melon Cantaloup
Frontignan
• • •
Consommé en Gelée
Velouté de Champignons à l'Italienne
• • •
Truite Saumonée Pochée au Vin d'Asti
accompagnée de Paupiettes de Sole à la Montpensier
• • •
Filet de Boeuf Poêlé à la Piemontaise
Petits Pois à la Française
Pommes Noisettes
• • •
Suprêmes de Volaille Royale Alliance
Pointes d'Asperges à la Crème
Aspic de Homard à la Parisienne
• • •
Cailles aux Feuilles de Vigne
Salade Victoria
• • •
Coeurs d'Artichauts à la Moelle
• • •
Pêches Princesse Louise d'Orléans
Friandises
• • •
Corbeille de Fruits
• • •
Café Moka
Liqueurs de France

Menu for the Dinner
Presided Over by the Prince of Wales

Melon Cantaloup

• • •

Tortue Claire Saint-Germain

• • •

Truite Saumonée Royale
Whitebait à la Diable

• • •

Mousse de Jambon au Velouté
Epinards au Beurre

• • •

Selle d'Agneau à la Broche
Haricots Verts à l'Anglaise
Pommes de Terre à la Crème

• • •

Suprêmes de Volaille en Gelée à l'Alsacienne

• • •

Cailles Souvarow
Salade de Blanc de Romaine

• • •

Asperges d'Argenteuil

• • •

Biscuit Glacé à l'Ananas
Fraises au Maraschino

• • •

Laitances
Café Turc

• • •

Vins: Amontillado
Milk–Punch
Berncasther Doctor, 1874
Brown Cantenac, 1888
Pommery Brut, 1884
Moët Cuvée, 1884
Château Léoville Poyferré (cachet du Château), 1878
Grande Fine, 1865
Groft's Old Port, 1858
Curaçao Marnier, Extra Sec

A Dinner in Red

In December 1895, a high-living group of young English gentlemen won the tidy sum of 350,000 francs betting on red at the roulette tables in Monte Carlo, and they decided to hold a banquet in honor of their favorite color. They asked the Savoy restaurant to carry out their dream.

Everything was red and gold except, of course, the chicken stuffed with truffles, where black momentarily replaced the red.

The table was decorated with petals of red roses. The menus were red. The chairs were red, and had the lucky winning number 9 stuck on them. The banquet room was decorated with palm trees to evoke the Riviera, and these were strung with red light bulbs. The effect was stunning; it brought to mind the evening passed in the vast casino built in Monte Carlo, that mysterious rock of luck and fortune.

Truffles reached their apogee in France in the nineteenth century when nearly every grand meal featured at least one dish that was bejeweled with the prized black diamond. Such liberal use of truffles today is impractical, not only because of their price but also because of diminished supplies. In 1892 two thousand tons of truffles were harvested in France; today only 25 to 150 tons are gathered annually.

The menu itself completed the fantasy:

Appetizer

Hors d´oeuvre *

Clicquot Rosé

• • •

Consommé au Fumet de Perdrix Rouges
Paillettes Dorées

• • •

Suprême de Rouget au Chambertin
accompagnés de Laitances de Carpes
aux Ecrevisses à la Bordelaise

• • •

Cailles Mascotte (quail was their mascot)
Riz Pilaf (de rigueur)
Château Lafite, Etampe 1870

• • •

Selle d'Agneau de Galles aux Tomates à la Provençale
Purée de Haricots Rouges
Sauce Souveraine au Suc de Pommes d'Amour
Château Lafite

• • •

Pluie d'Or[†]

• • •

Poularde Truffée aux Perles Noires du Périgord
Salade de Coeurs de Laitue Rouge des Alpes

• • •

Asperges Nouvelles
Sauce "Coucher de Soleil par un Beau Soir d'Eté"[††]

• • •

Parfait de Foie Gras
en Gelée au Paprika Doux à la Hongroise
Champagne: Cordon Rouge (Cuvée Spéciale)

---

* Open puff-pastry sandwiches of round slices of red smoked salmon (about 5 centimeters in diameter) were served with black caviar. One sandwich had the caviar under the salmon, the other the caviar on top. These appetizers were served on puff pastry cut into circles and presented on little red napkins.

† A dwarf mandarine tree, its base surrounded with chocolate coins decorated with gold spangles and mixed with tangarines; everything covered with a lace of spun sugar dyed gold.

†† Sauce "Sunset on a beautiful summer evening."

Rocher de Monte Carlo*

....

Assorted Mignardises for the Ladies
• • •
Café Mode Orientale
Grandes Liqueurs de France
Cigares

....

And if the guests at the end of the dinner were only moderately red in the face, it was due to the fine quality of the French red wines that we served to accompany this menu. These young Englishmen, delighted with their banquet, vowed to try their luck at the gambling tables once more. As we never heard from them again, I'm afraid that Lady Luck never showed up!

---

* An ice sculpture of the hill of Monte Carlo, lit up with red lights. At its base, red carnations and red autumn leaves surrounding a crystal bowl containing a *Mousse de Curaçao* covered with red strawberries macerated in sugar and Curaçao.

The Little Sisters of the Poor

DURING THIS PERIOD AT THE SAVOY, two nuns visited me every morning in a wagon pulled by a tired looking horse driven by one of the elderly pensioners of their old age home. They came to pick up coffee grounds that still retained some caffeine, tea leaves that had only been used once, and the crusts of bread left over from making toast.

I was touched by the admirable devotion of the Little Sisters of the Poor, who spent their entire existence trying to help the poverty-stricken.

I wanted to help them, and made sure that everything the hotel could donate to them was in good condition and clean. Some days I could add to their modest provisions the respectable gift of 150 to 200 quail left over from the previous night's dinner. Indeed, we removed the white meat from these quail to serve to our customers, but each carcass still had two legs on it! And in fact all the aroma so much appreciated by real lovers of game is actually found in the dark meat. These birds, prepared with rice according to my instructions, were delicious, and the old-age pensioners fully appreciated them. As this manna from heaven came to them regularly, they baptized those evenings "gala nights" and asked that we inscribe on their menu " Quail Pilaf *à la* Little Sisters of the Poor."

We took every care at the end of the meal that the leftover quail be placed in an enamel pail reserved for this purpose; it was then refrigerated. The next day I would give the pail to the sisters, who would return it to me emptied of its contents.

One day we learned that their poor horse had died, to everyone's great consternation. I guessed that replacing the animal would put a great financial load on the sisters. I asked the nuns to announce my visit to the rest home on the next day. At the appointed time, the Reverend Mother, a distinguished and kindhearted lady, thanked me for the interest I took in her mission and our contributions to the well-being of her pensioners. Then she told me her worries; she had a horse in mind that she could buy at a reasonable price, but she still lacked five pounds.

This modest sum was brought to her the very next day, and two days later a new horse drove the mission wagon.

The year had not gone by before it was my turn to ask a favor of the Mother Superior. An elderly cook who once had a certain renown in some of the best restaurants in Paris had ended up penniless in London. He was not in any shape to work, even in a secondary position in a kitchen brigade, and his future seemed very bleak. Refusing to leave a former colleague in such a miserable situation, I took him on my team, inventing a small job for him that gave him just enough to live on; but that could only be a temporary solution. I thought I might be able to find a place for him with the Little Sisters.

I went to see the Mother Superior and explained my problem. "I don't have any room for the moment," she said, "But never mind! We'll find room for your *protégé*!" And she added with a smile, "We owe you at least that much!"

Three days later our elderly colleague was taken in by the Little Sisters, and he was enchanted by this unexpected solution to his problems. He finished his life there in peace.

During my entire stay at the Savoy, and later during the twenty years I spent at the Carlton, I continued to help the Little Sisters as much as possible. Alas! When I left England for good, my successors forgot the Little Sisters. When I once visited them, years later, they told me how much they regretted my departure, for as of that day, quail had disappeared from their table, and their "gala dinners" were but a sweet memory from the past.

Of Englishmen and Frogs

THE FROG IS A SMALL AMPHIBIAN; one species lives in water and another on land. Frogs can be found nearly everywhere. There are especially many in Egypt, and storks feed off them regularly. In winter the frog sleeps, then wakes up in the springtime. Doctors in the Middle Ages were generally opposed to considering them edible, but everyone was not of that opinion, as there are recipes existing from that time. In some countries, like England, they are considered disgusting. In France, however, they are eaten regularly. They are especially appreciated in the fall, when they are quite fat and their flesh is more delicate. Frog has been a popular dish in Paris for over two centuries.

A Frenchman from Auvergne, named Simon, actually made a fortune for himself just by fattening up and selling frogs from his neighborhood.

Many can be found in Italian markets and in Germany. In France only the thighs are used, served with a white sauce or sautéed in butter or olive oil, seasoned with salt and pepper, a pinch of parsley, and a little lemon juice. For those who like it, a little garlic makes it even better.

The English sometimes amuse themselves with caricatures showing the typical Frenchman eating frogs. They even call us "the frog–eaters." However, in *History of the Isle of Dominica,* written by the Englishman Atwood, I found this sentence: "In Martinique frogs abound, and they are eaten regularly. The English and French both prefer them to chicken. They are served in soups and in fricassees."

If the English generally hate frogs, at least in their plates, the Prince of Wales was an exception to the rule. He loved French food, whether it was Parisian–style *haute cuisine* or the food of the common people. In this he shared the tastes of the Duke of Orléans, who loved all strange French food as well, including fattened frog, snails, and even *tripes à la mode de Caen.*

This controversy over the frog made me laugh, and I swore that one day during my stay at the Savoy I would find a way to make *Messieurs les Anglais* taste the animal. I soon had the perfect occasion.

A great banquet with a ball was to be held several days later. Many cold dishes, as varied as possible, were created to adorn the buffet, and one of the ones I proposed was baptized *Nymphes à l'Aurore* (Nymphs at Dawn).

A charming and brilliant crowd of elite guests paid great homage to this dish and devoured it with zest, never dreaming that they were eating the detestable frog legs.

After this small victory, *Messieurs les Anglais,* my friends, allow me to say that the French are not the only "frog-eaters" anymore!

Here is how I prepared my magical concoction. After cooking the frog legs in a highly seasoned *court-bouillon,* I let them cool and then coated them in a *chaud-froid* sauce with paprika. I placed them in a square platter, artistically placed blanched tarragon leaves on them here and there, and refrigerated the dish. Then I decorated it by covering it with a thin chicken jelly. The platters were served embedded in ice blocks, which were indispensable to maintaining the perfect temperature for this dish.

* * *

Let me say a few words about why I used the word "nymph" in my menu instead of "frog." I have often, on this occasion and others, been criticized by the press because of the titles I use for my creations.

At the time when I managed the restaurant of the Savoy, nobody would have dared to present a platter of frog legs at an English meal, and even less so at a gala banquet for 600 people comprising the elite of English society. For my frog legs to have the success they merited, it was necessary to rebaptize them!

King Edward VII, who was still the Prince of Wales at the time, was very much amused by the entire affair and asked me to prepare him some "nymphs" a few days later. This was not a novel dish for him; he was too much of a gourmet and a friend of France to disapprove of my culinary hoax.

Here are some other recipes for frog legs:

In a large casserole with low sides, melt two large spoonfuls of butter and add a spoonful of finely chopped onion. When the onion starts to brown lightly, add about 50 frog legs that have previously been washed, drained on a towel, and rolled in flour. Brown the legs for a few minutes. Add the seasoning—salt, freshly ground pepper, a pinch of ground nutmeg, and a glass of Madeira wine (or Vieux Frontignan)—cover the casserole, let it simmer for a few minutes to reduce the sauce, and then add 3 deciliters of fresh cream. Bring to a boil; thicken the sauce by adding 3 egg yolks mixed with 2 spoonfuls of cream. Serve immediately with a plate of thinly sliced toast.

To vary the taste of this dish, one can add, while the onion is browning, either a teaspoon of paprika or, according to taste, a spoonful of curry powder, just before adding the frog legs. In this case, it would be good to serve the platter with a dish of Indian-style rice (riz pilaf).

And now let me give you my secret recipe for *Grenouilles Cardinalisées*.

Choose frog legs that are as fat and white as possible. In a large casserole, melt 3 good spoonfuls of fresh butter, mix in 3 to 4 dozen well-drained frog legs, and season with salt, pepper, and a pinch of ground nutmeg. Cover the casserole and let it simmer for about 10 minutes. Add 36 shelled shrimp tails and 200 grams of fresh truffle, peeled and thinly sliced; add a spoonful of Fine Champagne and three spoonfuls of Madeira wine, heat through for several minutes, and mix in a Béchamel sauce that has been prepared beforehand using cream and a shrimp butter made with the shells of the shrimp. Place the entire mixture in a silver timbale or a low wide terrine, and decorate it with small eggs cooked *mollet* (not quite hard-boiled), one egg for each guest. Serve with a basket of hot, thinly sliced toast.

Even though some people do not like the idea of eating frog, it is sure that the flesh of this animal is healthy, light, and very digestible. It is of course necessary to buy frogs that live in clean water. The best can be found in Burgundy and in Bresse. These little animals also make an excellent refreshing bouillon.

Emile Zola and Provençal Cuisine

ZOLA CAME TO LONDON to study life in the poor neighborhoods of that city and, paradoxically, chose to stay at the Savoy Hotel.

His tastes and distinct partiality to the cuisine of Provence and Piedmont gave me several occasions to speak to the author of *Pot Bouille*. During our conversations, he took such pleasure in describing his favorite food, speaking of his weakness for various dishes with such conviction, that one would really have thought that he was actually sitting at the table in front of the delicious mutton *pot-au-feu* with stuffed cabbage *à la mode de Grasse* that he adored.

Zola also loved fresh sardines seasoned with salt, pepper, and olive oil, and then grilled over the embers of vine shoots. He spoke of how they were served in an earthenware dish that had been rubbed lightly with a garlic clove, sprinkled at the last minute with a mixture of parsley and oil from Aix. Indeed, sardines cooked in this way must really have had an unforgettable savor.

Emile Zola (1840–1902) French novelist. Inspired by his readings in social history and medicine, Zola applied scientific techniques and observations to the depiction of French society under the Second Empire, and wrote a vast series of novels in which the characters and their social milieus are presented in minute detail. His novel Pot-Bouille *penetrated the respectable façade of a bourgeois family.*

Zola loved *blanquette* with baby lamb *à la provençale* accompanied by saffron noodles, scrambled eggs with cheese, and white truffles from Piedmont, cut into thin slices and presented in a *vol-au-vent* puff pastry crust. He loved risotto with small game and black truffle; he loved the famous dish of polenta with white truffle that the Emperor Napoléon was also so fond of. And he loved a good cassoulet with tomato, eggplant, zucchini, and and green peppers prepared *à la Provençale*.

"When I think of it," he told me, "the memory of these country meals brings me back to my childhood spent in Aix-en-Provence. I also remember those delicious sweet *calissons* that we used to nibble in class."

We could draw up a list of all of Zola's culinary tastes. It might not add anything to the glory of this great writer, but it would at least have the advantage of helping us know more about him as a man.

The End of the Savoy
and the Beginning of the Ritz

DURING THE YEARS I spent at the Savoy Hotel in London (1890–1897), I was also able to participate in the opening of the Grand Hotel in Rome, which had just been built.

Following Ritz's advice, the directors of the Savoy Hotel took interest in this enterprise and created a company to manage the new luxury establishment. Ritz took over its management, with the assistance of Alphonse Pfyffer of the Hôtel National in Lucerne. I was put in charge of installing the kitchens and the restaurant and of choosing the necessary personnel.

The problem of choosing the kitchen staff was a delicate one. I had to take into account the very natural feelings of nationalism of my Italian colleagues and friends, and to avoid bad feeling, I made sure that half of the staff I hired was Italian and the other half French. I made one of my students, Mr. Jaspard, *chef de cuisine*, and everything worked out perfectly.

The opening of the Grand Hotel in Rome was a great success. Since then, other similar large hotels have opened, such as the Hotel Excelsior, where I also contributed indirectly to organizing the kitchen staff.

At nearly the same date, in 1895, and always in cooperation with Ritz and Echenard, I helped to open the Chalet du Mont Revard, which had an excellent restaurant and several rooms to rent. The opening of this chalet coincided with the opening of the rack railway taking travelers to the Mont Revard plateau, which dominated the beautiful valley of Aix-les-Bains and its wide lake.

My various trips to Rome enabled me to visit the museums, monuments, and churches of the Vatican, leaving me with unforgettable memories.

In 1897, after a disagreement, or rather a misunderstanding, between Mr. d'Oyly Carte, chairman of the board, and César Ritz, manager of the Savoy Hotel, we were forced to leave the enterprise into which we had put so much heart.

We had saved the Savoy from bankruptcy, brought it to the summit of glory, and given its shareholders the satisfaction they merited. It would have been possible for these gentlemen to solve their differences in everyone's interest and without anyone losing face. They would have none of it. We therefore had to leave, and for me, I must admit, it was temporarily a bitter disappointment, but this sadness was quickly dissipated by a lucky event that came just in time to put things into proper perspective. Time is often the best judge, and this was the case for us.

At that time the Carlton Hotel was under construction and just about finished. The board of directors of the Carlton immediately seized upon this mistake of the Savoy Hotel and contacted us to take over the direction of their new hotel. Ritz, Echenard, and I unanimously agreed to their advantageous proposition.

For myself, there was a question of personal pride in my choice. I did not want to leave England without having finished the task I had started at the Savoy Hotel, which was the expansion of French cuisine not only in England but throughout the world. The twenty years I spent at the Carlton Hotel gave me this great satisfaction, and I did not leave this hospitable country until May 1920. I have kept the best of memories of that time and of the people with whom I worked, people that I learned to fully appreciate.

In March 1897, therefore, we left the Savoy Hotel for good. Construction of the Carlton Hotel in London was not yet finished, however, and we could not start installing the rooms and kitchens right away. This delay was actually quite timely.

One of the reasons for the disagreement between the owner of the Savoy and César Ritz was the construction of the Ritz Hôtel in Paris. The Ritz was just about finished and, without further ado, we started taking care of furnishing it—the apartments, rooms, restaurant, kitchens, wine cellars, etc., including the services essential to an innovative hotel with all the modern comforts necessary to satisfy a demanding clientèle. We took care of this down to the last detail, and our efforts did not go unrecognized. Opened on June 5, 1898, the Ritz Hotel rapidly became the meetingplace for a wealthy clientèle from the highest French and foreign society.

Situated on Place Vendôme in the heart of Paris, the hotel had a unique location, protected from the noise of the streets, with calm and quiet ensured during the night. Its shaded garden allowed guests to lunch outdoors, which was very much appreciated during the hot summer months. At tea time the Ritz became the meeting place for the cream of society in France and abroad. Although newly constructed, its facade recalled the time of *Le Roi Soleil* (Louis XIV) and the *fleur-de-lys* of our historical France. The first floor was in the style of Louis XIV, and the dining room was Regency.

I would not like to forget to mention the devoted assistance of Mrs. Marie Ritz, who, after the death of her husband (during World War I), never ceased to participate in the development and improvement of this elegant hotel. She was a member of the board of administration and her views were most valuable. The presence of a woman in hotel administration is very important. Mrs. Ritz, thanks to her tact and fine taste, contributed greatly to maintaining the splendor of the enterprise created by her husband. I would like to recall that during World War I a part of this hotel was turned over to the Red Cross as a hospital for wounded French officers. And I want to emphasize again that the entire staff of the Hôtel Ritz is, and has always been, most exemplary.

Part Six

The Great Era of the Carlton

London
1899 – 1909

The Early Beginnings
of the Carlton

THE HÔTEL RITZ IN PARIS opened on June 5, 1898, and by March 1899 it was a complete success. Every service being fully operational, I left Paris and headed back to London.

The construction of the Carlton Hotel was finished, and it was time to take care of installing all the services required for a hotel with the most modern comforts. Once again, César Ritz proved that he merited his nickname of "King of Hosts." I was personally in charge of installing the kitchens and dining rooms.

The Carlton Hotel was inaugurated on July 1, 1899, and was like a rosebud that, barely open, already showed all of its beauty. In fact, the wings of our newborn grew so rapidly that other Carlton Hotels sprang up everywhere. I am sure that the aroma of the *suprêmes de perdreaux au parfum de truffe* and other such delicacies that I proposed helped to enhance its reputation as a new temple of gastronomy.

The discovery of gold and diamonds in the territories that made up South Africa caused the tension between the English settlers and the Dutch (known as Boers) to come to a head in the Boer War (1899–1902).

The twenty years I spent in this hotel were devoted to inventing new dishes to vary the menus and satisfy my gourmet clients, who were always on the lookout for new gastronomic sensations.

The opening of the Carlton Hotel took place at the same time as war broke out between England and South Africa over the Transvaal gold mines. Every evening several tables were sure to be reserved in the main restaurant for farewell dinners for officers leaving for the Transvaal. These very pleasant dinners, rendered full of gaiety by the officers' enthusiasm, were just a foretaste of the brilliant future to come for the Carlton. The initial success of the restaurant never ceased to grow, and it soon became the meeting place for the social elite. At the dinner hour, one could see there the richest people in England and the world, princes and princesses, dukes and duchesses, great barons of the banking world, political figures, ministers, and also great artists, writers, journalists, theatre stars, etc. It was not rare, on some nights, to see our charming lady customers bedecked in jewels worth millions, sparkling in the subdued lighting which had been carefully studied to enhance their complexions with a soft pink. Those were the good old days!

Palm Court was the dining hall at the Carlton Hotel, becoming famous when a rich patron threw a Venetian party and had guests sailed about in the water-filled dining room while they were being serenaded by an Italian singer.

The splendid banquets and dinners offered by the Carlton extended the fame of French cuisine abroad and helped to make our national products known and appreciated. The success we had known at the Savoy Hotel was only intensified at the Carlton. Most of our former customers followed us to the new hotel, particularly many brilliant actors and actresses whose tastes I often had the pleasure of satisfying.

The Story of *La Pêche Melba*

I FIRST PUT *Pêche Melba* on the menu for the opening of the Carlton Hotel. I had already met the great diva Nellie Melba when she stayed at the Savoy Hotel in 1893 and 1896, while she was singing at Covent Garden. I had had the great privilege of attending one of her performances of *Lohengrin*.

To show my great admiration and to thank her for the enchanting evening I had spent under the magic spell of her wonderful voice and undeniable talent as an actress, I wanted to create a surprise for her. The day after her performance, Mrs. Melba was to dine at the restaurant with a few friends, and I seized the occasion.

Commemorating the majestic mythical swan that appears in the first act of *Lohengrin*, I presented her with a dessert of peaches on a bed of vanilla ice cream, covered with a lace of spun sugar, and placed in a silver bowl nestled between the wings of a beautiful swan sculpted out of a large block of ice. The effect was stunning, and Madame Melba was delighted with my

Some say that Pêche Melba was the inspiration for the American ice cream sundae, and the New York Times wrote in Escoffier's obituary that "Pêche Melba is the feudal name for our democratic sundae."

creation. I saw the famous opera singer recently at the Hôtel Ritz in Paris, and she again spoke to me of that famous evening.

The success of that creation was rapid and conclusive. Twenty-seven years after the dessert appeared, it still has world wide renown, although I regret to say that the real recipe is too often changed.

Pêche Melba is a simple dish made up of tender and very ripe peaches, vanilla ice cream, and a purée of sugared raspberry. Any variation on this recipe ruins the delicate balance of its taste. Some take the liberty of replacing the raspberry purée with strawberry jam or red currant jelly. This alters the original taste completely. Even worse is the carelessness of some publishers who do not take the trouble of doing the proper research, and actually go and print the so-called "real" recipe, advising that arrowroot or some other floury substance be added to the raspberry. Others suggest decorating the peach with whipped cream. The results obtained have absolutely nothing to do with the original recipe and could hardly satisfy the palate of a real connoisseur.

Original Recipe for La Pêche Melba

(FOR 6)

Louis XVI was tremendously fond of peaches, which were nicknamed "téton de Venus" or "Venus's breast." Peaches first arrived in North America with the Spanish, and numerous native American tribes cultivated the fruit across the continent.

Choose 6 tender and perfectly ripe peaches. The Montreuil peach, for example, is perfect for this dessert. Blanch the peaches for 2 seconds in boiling water, remove them immediately with a slotted spoon, and place them in iced water for a few seconds. Peel them and place them on a plate, sprinkle them with a little sugar, and refrigerate them. Prepare a liter of very creamy vanilla ice cream and a purée of 250 grams of very fresh ripe raspberries crushed through a fine sieve and mixed with 150 grams of powdered sugar. Refrigerate.

To serve: Fill a silver timbale with the vanilla ice cream. Delicately place the peaches on top of the ice cream and cover with the raspberry purée. Optionally, during the almond season, one can add a few slivers of fresh almonds on top, but never use dried almonds.

Presentation: Embed the silver timbale in an ice sculpture and add a lace of spun sugar over the peaches (optional).

Note: Blanching the peaches in boiling water and immediately cooling them in iced water has the effect of keeping them fresh for several hours and preventing them from blackening, which is of great importance for large restaurants. If, however, it is necessary to keep the peaches until the next day, they must be placed in an earthenware dish and covered with boiling syrup.

Le Guide Culinaire

The first edition of the Guide Culinaire *was published in 1903. Today it is still regarded as a classic for professional chefs.*

IT WAS ALSO DURING the Carlton Hotel period that the first edition of my *Guide Culinaire* was published.

Several years before, I had spoken to Urbain Dubois about my idea of writing a practical guide for future chefs of large restaurants. The need for this kind of guide became more apparent every day to address the problems of rapid service now becoming current in these kinds of restaurants. Dubois actively encouraged me to carry out this project, but as I was very busy with my other activities, I started to write the *Guide* only in 1898.

When I returned to London for the opening of the Carlton, I again had to put off this project, and was only able to complete it in 1900, thanks to everyone's encouragement and especially the tenacity of my two collaborators,* without whose help I would never have been able to finish such a huge task.

* Philéas Gilbert and Emile Fétu. [ed.]

118

I didn't want the *Guide* to be a luxurious work of art or a curiosity that would be relegated to library shelves. I wanted it to be a work tool more than a book, a constant companion that chefs would always keep at their side. Although it contains more than 5,000 new recipes, I cannot pretend that it is exhaustive. Even if it were finished today, it would be out–of–date tomorrow, because progress never stops. The only thing we can do to remedy this is to constantly update it and add new recipes in each new edition.

I had been a long-standing friend of Urbain Dubois and Emile Bernard (both had been chefs at the court of King Wilhelm of Prussia) and therefore wanted to dedicate the book to their memory. I would have been lacking in a sacred duty had I forgotten to so honor my illustrious predecessors.

For contemporary chefs, the prestigious name of Urbain Dubois brings back memories of the elaborate and sumptuous dishes he proposed in *Cuisine Classique, Cuisine Artistique,* and the other cookbooks he published, either by himself or in collaboration with Emile Bernard. It is obvious, unfortunately, that this elaborate food is impossible to serve in today's world.

One of Dubois' greatest contributions was the important role he played in the growing use of the so-called service *à la russe,* that is to say the presentation of dishes one after the other, rather than the service *à la française* that was then popular, with all dishes being presented together at the beginning of the meal. The methods of restaurant service that he introduced and imposed were themselves changed and replaced during his lifetime by newer systems that corresponded better to the needs of the modern clientèle.

As representatives of an art form that necessarily reflected the tendencies and habits of a certain era, Urbain Dubois and Emile Bernard were clear-sighted enough to discern the needs of their times, courageous enough to break away from old practices that had become outdated, and persistent and tenacious enough to impose new methods better designed to meet modern needs.

I myself have often been forced to make profound changes in my restaurant service to meet the needs of the ultra rapid pace of modern life. For instance, I have had to eliminate pedestals and invent new, simplified ways of laying out and presenting dishes. To do this, I have even had to invent new restaurant equipment.

But the basics of cooking will remain the same as long as cooking exists. Simplifying it on the outside takes away none of its intrinsic value. At a time when all is undergoing modification and change, it would be foolish to claim to establish the future of an art which is connected in so many ways to fashion and is just as changeable.

In aiming my *Guide Culinaire* at young chefs who will be at the head of our profession in twenty years, it is my duty to recommend that they pay careful attention to the immortal works of our great masters as well as study all other culinary publications. A popular French saying goes *"On n'en sait jamais trop"*—the more one learns, more one realizes how much is left to learn. Studying opens up the horizons of the mind and is the best means of perfecting one's profession.

On the *Amerika*
with Emperor Wilhelm II

DURING THE YEARS 1904–1906, the navigation company Hamburg Amerika Line constructed its first luxury liner, the *Amerika*, for exclusive service between Hamburg and New York.

This floating palace had the most modern comforts, with sumptuous apartments and suites, and a restaurant serving French cuisine where first class passengers could dine *à la carte*, ordering their meals in advance and reserving their tables for the time of their choice. The kitchens were located next to the restaurant to facilitate service. The meals were prepared by a kitchen brigade of ten cooks under the orders of a *chef de cuisine*. During dinner, an excellent orchestra helped the passengers to forget that they were at sea. The restaurant had been most elegantly decorated by Sormani of boulevard Haussmann, Paris.

The Carlton Company in London accepted the offer to manage the restaurant, baptized the Ritz–Carlton Restaurant, and undertook the responsibility of installing the required equipment and hiring the necessary personnel. As I was the chef and restaurant manager, I was put in charge of carrying out these tasks.

The Amerika's maiden voyage was to begin on June 19, 1906. On June 18, the day before the liner was to sail from Cuxhaven, the Emperor of Germany, Wilhelm II, decided to visit the ship and dine on board. I was therefore asked to compose a menu worthy of our imperial guest.

Among the dishes on the menu was a *Mousse d'Ecrevisse*. The person charged with translating the menu into German got stuck on the word *mousse* and, looking the word up in a dictionary, found that it means "young sailor." I was asked if I truly believed Germans to be cannibals. I explained that the word *mousse*, in this case, means "something frothy"; it is a very common culinary term and a feminine noun in French, contrary to its homonym, meaning "apprentice sailor," which is a masculine noun in French. Therefore, one says "une *mousse à la fraise*" for strawberry mousse, and "un *mousse*" for the sailor.

After explaining fully, I added, "If I had served you a very tender young sailor, wouldn't he have been more appetizing than that old Bavarian* that has been on our menus for the last two centuries?" Everyone laughed at the joke, and finally we decided to leave the menu in French.

At seven o'clock precisely, the Emperor and his suite arrived from Kiel, where they had been attending sailing races, and sat down to dine. They had barely started the meal when one of his officers said to the Emperor, "Your Majesty brought Escoffier here especially from London. Did you know that he was a prisoner of war in 1870 and might well decide to poison us?"

I was immediately told of this remark, which could have had unpleasant consequences for me. Several seconds later, a huge devil of an officer strode into the kitchen, supposedly to have a look at the installation, but I suspected that the purpose of his visit was otherwise, for he asked me, "Is it true that you were a prisoner of war in 1870?"

*A very famous dessert, the Bavarois (or Bavarian cream) is a beautifully presented mold of custard sauce with gelatin, beaten egg whites, lightlty beaten cream, and a flavoring (e.g., fruit or chocolate). [ed.]

I replied, "Indeed, I was interned as a prisoner of war in the camp at Mainz, but I did not come here to poison you. You may dine in peace. If, one day, your country once again seeks war with France, and I am still able, I will do my duty. But for the time being, you may relax and not let anything trouble your digestion."

After the dinner, the Emperor wanted to visit the kitchen. I welcomed him with all the respect his imperial rank deserved. He proved to be very friendly. Right away he put me at my ease, and I answered all of his questions freely. He asked me, "Did I hear that in 1870 you were my grandfather's prisoner of war?" and then wanted to know where I had been captured, where I had been interned, and whether or not I had been well-treated as a prisoner.

"I cannot say that 'well–treated' is quite the right word. Personally, I cannot say that I had too much to complain about. But all around me I saw the inhuman consequences of fratricidal wars. We can be German, French, English or Italian...but why make war? When one thinks of the crimes that are committed, of the widows, of the orphans, of the crippled and the maimed, of the poor women abused by invading forces, one cannot help but tremble with indignation."

The Emperor listened to me and smiled. "I regret," he replied, "that I was not there. I would have freed you."

"I very much appreciate Your Majesty's solicitude, but it would have taken an act of God for Your Majesty to ever have met me."

Then we spoke of cooking. The Emperor took great pleasure in explaining to me how his menus were prepared. For his breakfast he had adopted an English menu, with coffee or tea with cream, fried eggs and bacon, kidneys, chops, steaks, grilled fish, and fruit. For lunch, a more copious meal, but for dinner a very light meal so as not to overcharge the stomach and to keep a head for the social conversations necessary in high society.

The Emperor left the restaurant at around ten o'clock, and the next morning, right after breakfast, he left the boat to return to Berlin. I wished him a pleasant trip and, shaking my hand, he said, "Good-bye, and I hope to see you again soon."

Menu Served to Emperor Wilhelm II

Hors-d'oeuvre Suédois
Potages
Consommé en Gelée
Tortue Claire
• • •
Suprêmes de Sole au Vin du Rhin
• • •
Selle de Mouton de Pré-salé aux Laitues à la Grecque
Petits Pois à la Bourgeoise
• • •
Poularde au Paprika Rose Gelée au Champagne
• • •
Cailles aux Raisins
Coeurs de Romaine aux Oeufs
• • •
Asperges Sauce Mousseline
Ecrevisses à la Moscovite
• • •
Soufflé Surprise
Friandises
• • •
Fruits
Pêches, Fraises, Nectarines
Raisins Muscats
• • •
Café Mode Orientale
• • •
Vins: Eitchbacher 1897
Château Fourteau 1888
Liedricher Berg
Anslese 1893
Château Rauzan Ségla 1878
Veuve Clicquot
Ponsardin rosé
Heidseick & Co. 1900
Fine Champagne
La Grande Marque de l'Empereur

The Grand Hôtel in Monte Carlo, c.1895. (Copyright Roger-Viollet)

The Hotel Cecil (left) and the Savoy Hotel (right) in London, in 1900, seen from the Victoria Embankment, with typical London taxis of the time. (Copyright Roger-Viollet)

Arrival of royalty at the Hotel Ritz in Paris, Place Vendôme, c.1930.
(Photo Courtesy of Claude Mille)

The Carlton Hotel, London, c.1900.

César Ritz (1850-1918)
(Photo Courtesy of Claude Mille)

Kaiser Wilhelm II of Germany (1859–1941)
(Copyright Roger-Viollet)

Albert Edward, Prince of Wales (1841-1910) coronated in 1901 as King Edward VII of Great Britain & Ireland (1901-1910).
(Photo Courtesy of UPI/Corbis-Bettman)

Adelina Patti, Italian opera singer (1843-1919).
(Copyright Roger-Viollet)

Nellie Melba (1859-1931)

Sarah Bernhardt (1844-1923)

Charles Scotto, chef of the Hôtel Pierre, c.1930, presenting Pêche Melba.

A typical restaurant dining room at the turn of the century. (Copyright Roger-Viollet)

Auguste Escoffier with his kitchen brigade at the Carlton Hotel in London (1908).
(Photo Courtesy of Claude Mille)

The kitchen brigade at the inauguration of the Hotel Pierre, October 1, 1930, with Escoffier, Mr. Pierre, and Charles Scotto.

Escoffier's menu from the Savoy Hotel, October 30, 1895.

Menu proposed by Escoffier for the gala dinner that was to be held at the Carlton Hotel on June 24, 1902, in honor of the coronation of King Edward VII.

Typical menu presentation at the turn of the century.

My First Trip to the United States

The Success of *Prix Fixe* Menus at the Carlton

SOME TIME AFTER MY CONVERSATION WITH THE EMPEROR, the Hamburg Amerika Line, in concert with the directors of the Ritz-Carlton Hotel, decided to make a few improvements on the liner *Deutschland* by adding a grill room at the front of the ship. They asked for my professional opinion and offered me a round-trip voyage between Southampton and New York in order to study the question. I was delighted, and made the trip in March 1907. My report was unfavorable with regard to the project of installing a grill room there, since the ship's pitching and tossing would have made it impossible to eat in peace.

I informed the captain of the *Deutschland* of my opinion, and he agreed with me. However, the middle of the liner was extremely stable. This was my first ocean voyage, and I never missed a meal in the main dining room, finding myself as comfortable there as in any restaurant on land. Thanks to this trip, I was able to spend eight days in New York and had the chance to visit many old friends.

I was staying at the newly opened Knickerbocker Hotel as the guest of its owners, Mr. and Mrs. Regan. They had come to London shortly before opening their hotel to recruit high-quality personnel. They had stayed at the Carlton Hotel and had asked me to recommend an excellent *chef de cuisine* and other good cooks, which I did with pleasure. To make sure they would be satisfied, I even recommended my own assistant chef at the Carlton, Mr. Gastaud, along with other trusty members of my kitchen staff. I later congratulated myself on my choices, because Mr. Regan was fully satisfied and gave me many compliments on Mr. Gastaud and his collaborators.

I returned to the Carlton Hotel after a three-week absence. The Easter vacations were over and London's high season had begun. The sumptuous dinners and late–night suppers that were famous at the restaurant during the months of May, June, and July gave the Carlton all of its usual glamour, thanks to the sympathy and friendliness of its faithful clientèle. I therefore turned my attention to the art of *haute cuisine* and the invention of the new and spectacular dishes that encouraged my clients to come back time and again.

The system of *prix fixe* meals for a table of at least four that we had offered at the Savoy proved to be just as popular when we offered it at the Carlton.

Here are a few examples of *prix fixe* menus that we served:

JUNE 1901

Menu @ 12 shillings 6

(4 COVERS)

Melon Cocktail
Velouté Saint–Germain
• • •
Truite de Rivière Meunière
• • •
Blanc de Poulet Toulousain
Riz Pilaf
• • •
Noisette d'Agneau à la Moelle

126

Haricots Verts à l'Anglaise
Pommes Byron
• • •
Cailles en Gelée à la Richelieu
Salade Romaine
Asperges d'Argenteuil au Beurre Fondu
• • •
Mousse Glacée aux Fraises
Friandises

SEPTEMBER 1901

Menu @ 17 shillings 6

(8 COVERS)

Grapefruit au Kirsch
Saumon Fumé
• • •
Consommé Royal
Crème de Champignons au Curry
• • •
Timbale de Sole Carlton
Whitebaits Diables
• • •
Jambon de Prague sous la Cendre
Concombre au Paprika Rose
• • •
Mignonnettes de Poulet en Gelée à l'Alsacienne
Grouse à la Broche
• • •
Bread Sauce
Salade Rachel
• • •
Poires Montmorency
Macarons de Nancy

July 1901

Menu @ 15 shillings 6

(8 COVERS)

Melon Cantaloup au Porto

• • •

Consommé en Gelée Madrilène
Rossolnie à la Crème

• • •

Turbotin au Chambertin
Noisettes de Ris de Veau Favorite
Petits Pois à l'Anglaise

• • •

Selle d'Agneau de Galles Poêlée
Laitues Farcies à l'Orientale
Pommes de Terre Anna

• • •

Suprêmes de Volaille Jeannette
Salade d'Asperges aux Oeufs

• • •

Pêches Melba
Gaufrettes Bretonnes

DECEMBER 1901

Menu @ 1 guinea

(20 COVERS)

Caviar Frais
Crêpes au Blé Noir
Huîtres Natives

• • •

Tortue Claire au Frontignan
Velouté Princesse Mary
Paillettes Dorées

• • •

Homard Carmélita
Riz Créole
Eperlans à l'Anglaise

• • •

Selle de Chevreuil Grand Veneur
Crème de Marrons
Sauce Aigre–Douce au Raifort

• • •

Parfait de Foie Gras en Gelée au Champagne

• • •

Punch à la Romaine
Poularde Périgourdine
Salade de Laitues au Oeufs

• • •

Cocurs d'Artichauts à la Moelle
et Pointes d'Asperges au Beurre

• • •

Ananas Glacé à l'Orientale
Mignardises Gourmandes

A Royal Banquet

Menu and Recipes

THE FOLLOWING BANQUET was prepared for the gala planned to be held at the Carlton Hotel on June 24, 1902, in honor of the coronation of His Majesty Edward VII, King of England and Ireland. I have included a few of my recipes.

Caviar Frais Melon Cantaloup

• • •

Consommé aux Nids d'Hirondelles

• • •

Velouté Royal aux Champignons Blancs
Paillettes au Parmesan

• • •

Mousseline de Sole Victoria

• • •

Poularde Edouard VII
Concombres au Curry

• • •

Noisettes d'Agneau de Galles Souveraine
Petits Pois à l'Anglaise

• • •

Suprêmes de Caneton de Rouen en Gelée

• • •

Neige au Clicquot

• • •

Ortolans au Suc d'Ananas
Blanc de Romaine aux Oeufs

• • •

Coeurs d'Artichauts Favorite

• • •

Pêches Alexandra
Biscuit Mon Désir
Mignardises

• • •

Café Mode Orientale

• • •

Les Vins et Liqueurs au Choix des Dîneurs

Mousseline de Sole Victoria

Ingredients: One 1-kilo filet of sole, 5 egg whites, 1 1/2 liters fresh cream, 10 grams salt, 3 grams white pepper.

Season the sole and crush the flesh with a pestle. Add egg whites little by little. Strain through a fine sieve. Place the mixture in a well–plated *sauteuse* (shallow casserole) and place on ice to cool for two hours.

Add the cream a little at a time, working it in gently with a wooden spoon, until the entire quantity has been incorporated.

Mousselines are molded with a large soup spoon, just like large oval quenelles, and poached just like quenelles, but much more care must be taken with them. Place them carefully in a buttered frying pan and cover them gently with salted boiling water (10 grams of salt per liter). Cover the pan and maintain a gentle simmer for 12 to 19 minutes. Be sure not to let the water boil!

The coronation of King Edward VII was to be held on June 24, 1902, and members of society's highest elite were coming from all over the world to attend this event. Every room in the Carlton Hotel had been reserved and Ritz and Escoffier had been working feverishly for weeks to plan the celebration, especially the huge formal gala banquet to be held that night. Just two days before the ceremony, the new king had to undergo an emergency operation, and the coronation was postponed indefinitely. Hundreds of cancellations poured into the Carlton. For Ritz, it was an appalling shock, and led to a mental and physical breakdown from which he never fully recovered. The coronation was held two months later, on August 9, 1902.

Drain the *mousselines*, place them in a shallow serving platter, and cover them with the following sauce: mix together a sufficient amount of diced cooked lobster meat, 1/3 of the same amount of diced truffle, and a fine creamed lobster butter sauce.

La Poularde Edouard VII

Stuff a pullet (fattened chicken) with 200 grams of rice pilaf prepared with 130 grams of diced truffle and *foie-gras*. Poach it in a white veal stock for 55 to 60 minutes, according to the size of the fowl. Serve coated with a curry sauce to which has been added 130 grams of diced red pepper per liter of sauce (red capsicum can be found preserved in 1-pint jars on the market). Serve a garnish of creamed cucumbers separately.

Noisettes d'Agneau de Galles Souveraine

Lamb *noisettes* are the choicest pieces of meat cut from the fillet or the neck of the lamb; in the latter case, only the first 6 or 7 ribs are used.

Prepare toasts fried in butter. Sauté the noisettes in clarified butter, place them on croutons, and nap with the following sauce: 1 part Béarnaise sauce, 1/4 part meat glaze, 1/4 part tomato sauce. Surround with potato nuggets about the size of an olive, cooked in butter.

Suprêmes de Caneton de Rouen en Gelée au Frontignan

Choose a fair-size *caneton de Rouen* (Rouen duckling) and roast it, making sure to keep it underdone, still a little rare and cold. Remove the breasts and divide them each into three slices. Place the slices on a plate and cool.

Put aside the duck's liver. Crush the rest of the carcass with a pestle and place in a saucepan with a small glass of Armagnac and a glass of Burgundy wine (not too aged). Cook to reduce the sauce to 1/3 its volume. Add 4 deciliters of demi–glace stock, boil for a few minutes, strain through a sieve, and place the resulting mixture in a terrine.

Sauté the duck's liver over a high flame with 7 or 8 poultry livers; season with salt, pepper, spices, a small spoonful of minced onion, and parsley. Push the livers through a fine sieve and put the resulting purée into a saucepan. Incorporate the wine sauce and 230 grams of butter using a wooden spoon; keep the purée away from heat and cold until it is smooth and homogenous.

Pour 3/4 of this purée into a crystal bowl or a square serving dish, place the cooked duckling breasts on top and hide them with a thin coating of the rest of the purée. Place 3 cooked cherries on top of each breast. Cover completely with an aspic made with Frontignan. Keep cold over ice.

To serve, place a bed of crushed ice on a large platter, covered with a folded napkin. Embed the dish of duckling breasts in this crushed ice and serve.

Coeurs d'Artichauts Favorite

Choose very fresh medium–size artichokes. Remove the first 3 rows of tough leaves and cut the other leaves horizontally to remove the hard ends. Do not remove the hairy chokes of the artichoke hearts until after they have been cooked. Round off the bottom of the artichoke hearts, sprinkle them with lemon juice, and cook them in salted water to which 2 spoonfuls of flour have been added.

As soon as they are cooked, drain them, remove the chokes, and garnish the hearts with diced truffle in a hot Béchamel sauce. Cover the artichokes lightly with the same sauce, sprinkle with grated cheese, and pour melted butter on top.

Arrange the hearts in a decorative rosette motif on a round ovenproof platter and put it briefly in a hot oven to set a light gratin *à la salamandre*.

A decorative bouquet of green asparagus tips cooked in butter and placed symmetrically over each artichoke heart will complete the exquisite harmony of this dish.

Pêches Alexandra

Choose perfectly ripe white peaches. Blanch them for three seconds in boiling water and then plunge them in icy water; skin them immediately. Place them in a terrine, sprinkle them with Kirsch and Marasquin, cover them with a boiling vanilla–flavored syrup and let them cool completely.

Place the peaches in a timbale containing a layer of vanilla ice cream covered with a strawberry purée. Embed the timbale in crushed ice.

Sprinkle the peaches with white and red rose petals and veil the whole with spun sugar.

Menu Served to Monseigneur le Duc d'Orléans

HERE IS THE MENU of a dinner for ten served to Monseigneur le Duc d'Orléans at the Carlton Hotel in London in October 1905, when he had just returned from his most interesting 1904 cruise to Spitzberg aboard the yacht *Maroussia*.

Caviar Perlé
Crèpes au Blé Noir

• • •

Consommé à la d'Orléans
Crème de Champignons au Paprika Rose
Paillettes Dorées

• • •

Truite Saumonée Pochée au Vin Blanc de Touraine Accompagnée de Queues
d'Ecrevisses en Coquilles Enrobée de Sauce Béchamel et Légèrement Gratinée

• • •

Selle de Chevreuil Grand Veneur
Sauce Venaisone
Purée de Patates Douces
Haricots Verts Frais à l'Anglaise

• • •

Poularde Sainte–Alliance
Coeurs de Romaine aux Oeufs

• • •

Asperges de Serre au Beurre Fondu

• • •

Poires Petit Duc
Sablés Viennois
Café Mode Orientale Liqueurs
Vieille Chartreuse du Couvent
Grande Fine Champagne

• • •

Vins: Chablis 1902
Ch. Mouton Rothschild 1899
Moët et Chandon Dry Impérial 1900

La Poularde Sainte-Alliance

(SERVES 8)

Carefully clean and peel 8 large truffles, heat them in butter, season them with salt and freshly ground pepper, add a glass of aged Madeira, and let them macerate in a tightly covered jar for 8 to 10 minutes.

Choose a nice fair-size pullet (fattened chicken), stuff it with the truffle mixture, and sauté the pullet in a *poêle* (French frying pan) so that it will be ready just in time for serving. When the pullet is nearly ready, rapidly cook as many ortolans* as there are guests and sauté in butter the same number of slices of *foie gras*. Send these to the table at the same time as the pullet accompanied by the pullet's juices strained and placed in a small vegetable saucepan so that it can be reheated rapidly and served boiling.

In the restaurant the *maître d'hôtel*, surrounded by three waiters, has at his disposal a hot portable stove placed on a serving table. When the pullet arrives, he rapidly separates the breasts and cuts

---

* Ortolans are a kind of small bird in the finch family. Found in England, they are prized as a table delicacy. [ed.]

them into slices while one waiter prepares one slice of *foie gras* on each warmed plate. The *maître d'hôtel* places one slice of pullet on the *foie gras* and surrounds it with the truffle stuffing. The plate is passed to the second waiter, who adds one ortolan and a spoonful of hot meat juice. The third waiter immediately places the garnished plates in front of the guests.

The pullet is thus served very rapidly and under the exact conditions necessary to enhance the exotic taste of this dish.

Note: The name *"Saint–Alliance"* that I gave to this culinary concoction, and which Brillat–Savarin also used in his *Physiology of Taste* to designate a famous toast, seemed to me to be the best name for a dish in which are the veritable jewels of *haute cuisine*: the breasts of a fine chicken, *foie gras*, ortolan, and truffle.

This dish was created at the Carlton Hotel in London and served a second time at a dinner for eight given by a Maharajah who was devoted to England.

Poires Petit Duc

Choose perfectly ripe medium-size pears (Comice or Duchess), peel them, and cook them in a light vanilla syrup. Let them cool in their syrup. Separately, prepare a chestnut ice cream lightly flavored with rum or Kirsch.

Cover the bottom of a crystal bowl with the chestnut ice cream. Place the drained pears in a crown and surround them with Bar–le–Duc red currants. In the center of the crown, place a mountain of whipped cream Chantilly.

Menu in Honor of
Sarah Bernhardt

THE FOLLOWING SUPPER was offered at the Carlton Hotel in London in honor of Sarah Bernhardt after her opening in *The King of Rome* at the Majesty Theater. The dinner was accompanied by *Moët et Chandon* champagne, divine Sarah's preferred wine.

Menu

(FOR 6)

Caviar Gris de Sterlet
Crèpes Mousseline
• • •
Consommé Madrilène en Tasse
Paillettes Dorées
• • •
Soufflé au Parmesan accompagné de Crevettes Roses Enrobées d'un Fin Velouté
au Paprika Rose Doux
• • •

138

Mignonnettes d'Agneau de Lait Mireille
Emincé de Truffes à la Crème
Petits Pois Frais à l'Anglaise
• • •
Suprêmes de Poularde aux Ortolans Sarah Bernhardt
en Gelée au Frontignan
• • •
Salade Favorite
• • •
Mandarines Glacées aux Perles des Alpes
Frivolités Féminines
• • •
Fruits
Raisins Muscats Pêches du Cap
• • •
Café Moka Liqueurs de France
• • •
Vins: Chablis
Château Lafite
Champagne Moët et Chandon

Soufflé aux Crevettes Roses au Paprika Doux

Choose 300 grams of very fresh small pink shrimp, remove their shells, and place them in a casserole with a big spoonful of butter. Heat them slightly and add a thin paprika sauce. Keep warm.

Separately, prepare a parmesan cheese soufflé mixture and cook it in a buttered soufflé timbale, timing carefully so that it can be served hot immediately. Bring the soufflé and the warm shrimp sauce to the table at the same time but in separate dishes. Optionally, one can add 2 spoonfuls of whipped cream to the shrimp sauce at the last minute.

Mignonnettes d'Agneau de Lait Mireille

Choose baby milk-fed lamb, with white flesh, well fattened. From the neck of the lamb cut out the smallest *mignonnette* cutlets, 2 per guest, and season them with salt; coat them lightly first in flour, then in beaten egg, and finally in freshly prepared white bread crumbs. Keep cold.

139

At the same time, start preparing the *émincé de truffes à la crème* that will be served at the same time. Choose excellent fair–size very black truffles, peel them carefully, cut them into thin slivers, and put them into a wide casserole. Add an equal amount of melted meat glaze, season moderately with salt and pepper, cover the casserole, and set it aside.

Fifteen minutes before serving, cook the cutlets in clarified butter. Heat the truffle for several seconds over a very low flame, add 3–4 spoonfuls of Béchamel sauce and enough boiling cream to cover the truffle; boil for 2 minutes. It is most important that the cream be very fresh, with no hint of an aftertaste.

Place the *mignonnette* cutlets on a warmed platter and cover them lightly with the following sauce: melt 3 spoonfuls of meat glaze with 3 spoonfuls of water, boil for 2–3 minutes and incorporate twice its volume of very fine butter and a little lemon juice. Note that if the butter separates from the meat glaze, it is possible to obtain the proper consistency again by adding 1 or 2 spoonfuls of boiling water.

Serve the cutlets with the *émincé de truffes* and a dish of garden peas *à l'anglaise.*

Suprêmes de Poularde aux Ortolans

Poach a pullet (fattened chicken) in a white veal stock (made by boiling 1 kilogram of veal hock and a veal trotter); remove the breasts and let cool. Divide each breast into 4 slices, trim them to an oval shape, and coat them with a white *chaud–froid* sauce. Place a large sliver of truffle on each breast. Keep cold.

Separately, choose 12 very fresh and fattened ortolans, pluck them, clean them carefully, and poach them 6–7 minutes in a brown veal stock *au champagne*. Let them cool in the stock. (*Note:* In England, during the season, it is always possible to find very fine live ortolans.)

With the cooking juices of the fowl, prepare an aspic jelly flavored with Frontignan wine.

To serve: Embed a large square platter in a block of ice and pour a thin layer of jelly on the bottom. As soon as the jelly has set, place on the platter 8 slices of perfect *foie gras* cut to the same size as the slices of pullet; add 1 slice of pullet on top of each slice of *foie gras* and arrange the ortolans in between the pullet–*foie gras* slices. Cover the entire dish with the rest of the aspic. To bring to the table, place the block of ice on a silver tray protected by a folded napkin.

Note: The square silver platter could be replaced by a crystal bowl.

Salade Favorite

This salad is composed of 2 parts asparagus tips, one part freshly cooked artichoke hearts cut into slivers, and several very fresh mushrooms, peeled and cut into slivers.

Seasoning: Mix together 4 spoonfuls of olive oil, 1 spoonful of wine vinegar, salt, pepper, a spoonful of paprika, and the yolks of 2 hard-boiled eggs, passed through a sieve.

The salad is served in a large salad bowl or crystal bowl.

Mandarines aux Perles des Alpes

Find as many tangerines as possible that still have their stalks with leaves and a thick skin that make them easier to empty. Cut off the top of the tangerines with a round, even cutter so as to remove a roundel of the peel with the stalk and 2 leaves still attached.

Empty the tangerines and garnish them inside with tangerine mousse mixed with little green Chartreuse bonbons. Cover with the roundel caps. With a brush, sprinkle the rinds of the fruit with water and place them in a refrigerator. As soon as the tangerines are coated with frost, serve them on a napkin covering a round platter embedded in crushed ice, surrounded by decorative green leaves.

Part Seven

The Consecration

Works and Voyages
1909 – 1930

My Professional Jubilee

FRIENDS AND COLLEAGUES IN LONDON, wanting to celebrate the fiftieth anniversary of my professional life, created a committee to make sure the festivities would be as glamorous as possible. Without telling me, they asked for donations, and planned to use the sum obtained to buy a work of art which would be offered to me in memory of the occasion.

Having counted all the donations, a member of the Committee, Mr. Espezel, came to me with great joy to announce that about 6000 francs had been collected; he asked me what I would like most to be done with it. Without hesitation I replied that what would please me most would be that the sum be donated to the Maison de Retraite de Duguy, an old–age home founded by Mr. Marguery for elderly chefs with no means of survival. "It would be a great pleasure for me to know that your generosity toward me will have served to ease the days of one of our colleagues, ensuring him bed and board in his old age."

To this donation I also added my own contribution in the form of a number of lottery tickets for shares in the Panama Canal, in the hope that the chance of winning could improve the fate of some of our old people.

The Maison de Retraite de Duguy no longer exists, but it has been replaced by the Mourier Foundation in Cormeilles-en-Parisis.

On October 23, 1909, the night of my jubilee at the Monico Restaurant, tables were set up from one end of the International Hall to the other, and the room was crowded with guests. After dinner, toasts were made to the King's health, to the royal family, and to the President of the French Republic, and Mr. Tresneau gave the following speech:

Last year in this same hall we raised our glasses to toast you as the world's best champion of French culinary art, and you told us of your intention to invite us to celebrate your professional jubilee this year. It was immediately obvious to us, your friends and colleagues, that it was rather up to us to congratulate you and tell you of how grateful we are to you for having worked so hard for half a century to spread the renown of our fine traditional French cuisine far and wide.

Among all the famous names in the world of culinary art from the end of the nineteenth century and the beginning of this one, yours stands out in a place of its own, at the top of the list, and this is due to your unremitting efforts, and to your tireless search for new resources to help our profession develop, stay up-to-date, and satisfy the requirements of an increasingly-demanding clientèle.

There is not one area in the complex domain of food that you have not fully researched, studied, and scrutinized with all the concentration and care that you bring to everything you do. This is why, practically without your realizing it, your fame grew and spread at the same time that your reputation became established throughout the world.

Thanks to you, the renown of French cuisine developed rapidly in this country and many others all over the world, and many French cooks were able to find jobs that they never would have obtained otherwise. Others are indebted to you for giving them, through your books, the principles guiding the basis of modern cooking, enabling workers who never had the good luck to work under your orders to keep up with the progress that you have brought to this art.

In my extemporaneous reply, I told them how touched I was by the sympathy and friendship that they had just shown me. This consecration was my reward for all my efforts in the last fifty years. Then I gave a brief *résumé* of my career, recognizing the fact that I had sometimes been criticized. But I pointed out that critics are quick to demolish ideas without ever proposing a better way to solve problems. I know that acts and words must be judged with proper measure, and one must keep in mind only one's moments of triumph.

I pointed out that I often heard that *haute cuisine* was in a state of decadence, but that I had noticed that such words often came from people whose great need to talk often forced them to pronounce opinions on subjects about which they had not the slightest notion. I confirmed that, far from falling into decadence, the art of cooking was growing and becoming finer every day. It is true that our stomachs do not have the same capacity to eat that they seemed to have in days gone by, but we chefs are here to take care of the necessary changes and adapt ourselves to evolving customs. And I stated my conviction that the modern cook has nothing to envy in his predecessors.

When the speeches were over, the board of directors of the Carlton Hotel presented me with a magnificent silver cup.

An Important Subject
The Suppression of Poverty

Escoffier published his ideas on the suppression of poverty in 1910, at about the same time that England was creating legislation that would lead to a welfare state. In 1913 several important London hotels and restaurants, including the Savoy, experienced strikes organized by their cooks and waiters who wanted a change in the long hours, unsanitary conditions, and lack of holiday time.

AT THE BEGINNING OF 1910 I published a small pamphlet on a project of mutual assistance to suppress poverty. I feel that most socialist theories on the matter, even the most far-fetched, are basically indisputable and just. But none of the great modern apostles have found a formula comparable to the simple one that revolutionized the ancient world: "Love thy neighbor as thyself."

If all men were fully aware of their duty, this beautiful maxim would be applied on a daily basis, and poverty would no longer exist. Already the beneficial effects of mutual insurance systems have begun to modify social conditions, but obviously the poorest of the poor cannot yet participate in these improvements. It is of these people we must think; it is for them that we must provide.

Furthermore, it would be possible today to organize an insurance system that would normally function without unduly taxing an already heavy budget, and that would enable society to provide for the old age of all the decent people who have worked hard all their lives without ever being able to save for their retirement.

To this end, everything is still left to be invented, including the very conception of the system, for the limited retirement funds proposed by our Chambers of Commerce last year are only a drop in the bucket toward helping the elderly that have been worked to the bone all their lives. It is not charity that we owe our industrially disabled, but a true pension, the same in all respects that we give to our disabled soldiers. Who would dare contest today that blue-collar workers are in the service of their country just as much as civil servants are? Most of them would probably have preferred to have jobs in a big administration which ensured them a decent retirement for less difficult and better paid work. They often find themselves shunted aside for lack of a proper education, or for lack of the political recommendations that play such an important role in finding work in our administrations, or simply because they are blessed with that spirit of independent enterprise that is one of the best qualities of the Frenchman. Must they suffer until their last dying day for want of schooling, for not having begged protection from those currently in power, or for having had enough confidence in themselves to want to take advantage of their youth and freedom?

There is no good reason not to assign a pension to these retired workers that is just as much their legitimate due as the pension allotted to civil servants. They both have a title that supersedes all others: they are members of humanity.

Having established this, it would seem most natural to create an old-age pension system with funds automatically provided for in the national budget, as they are for the military and the civil service. But I foresee a slew of objections, of which the primary and only valid one would be the crushing cost of such an innovation. And yet, a country that allots millions a year to maintaining its army and navy should logically be able to ensure a tranquil retirement to the very children who proudly give up their best years, and even their lives, when asked to defend it.

In fact, can't the powers–that–be see that the billions spent annually by each country to maintain an "armed peace," these billions that each year's budgets raise by the million, will soon cause such a tax surcharge on their

Similar national strikes in the docks, railways, and mines had already broken out throughout the country in 1911 and 1912. In France, a fully comprehensive social security program would not be adopted until 1928.

populations that the countries will have no choice but to make war? Well-spoken assurances of exaggerated pacifism bear little weight with me, for I know that even a leader truly believing in peace would have no chance of stopping events from following their fatal course. Hunger brings the wolf out of the forest just as fast as it brings the sword out of its scabbard. And just as the wolf needs no excuse to devour the lamb, certain politicians need no real reason to decree their carnage—they just make up a reason (for example, the falsified telegram that led to the 1870 war).

And yet, alongside noisy pacifists, there are men today all over the world who are truly wise and conscious of human rights and who are sincerely struggling for a better understanding among all countries. These men are probably a majority in all parliamentary bodies, and in any case surely make up their elite.

Why don't we at least try to found the basis for the famous European Confederation that the greatest thinkers of the last half–century have proclaimed a necessity? The vital interests of all countries are the same today: they all want peace first and foremost—not this "armed peace" that is only a hypocritical preparation for war, but a real and long–lasting peace.

There was a time when the local squires of two neighboring villages would put the countryside to fire and the sword to defend what they called their rights. Later, it would be two neighboring provinces that would declare stupid and relentless wars. When provinces united to become nations, it was the nation that declared war on its rivals. And we are still at that stage, in a century where marvelous industrial progress has long abolished the illusion of distance, in an era when travel has become so easy and so common that each country seems to be an extension of the next one. Why not come together, therefore, to form one large confederation, without, for that matter, needing to change in any way the constitutions that the various peoples have democratically chosen for themselves? We will end up doing it anyway, one of these days, and soon, but perhaps only after having gone through the most absurd and terrifying of all wars. Why can't the voice of reason make itself heard right now? The billions spent needlessly today could serve to ensure the rest and welfare of all our elderly as well as to bring an enormous improvement to the situation of the working class everywhere.

New York - Sarah Bernhardt
Le Carnet d'Epicure
The Fire at the Carlton

1910-1911

IN JULY 1910, the construction of the Ritz-Carlton Hotel in New York was nearly finished, and I was put in charge of installing its kitchens and hiring a highly competent *chef de cuisine* and the rest of the kitchen staff.

The inauguration of the hotel was to take place at the end of November and I had to get to New York a month earlier to make arrangements for the gala dinner, to ensure that the brigade of cooks, pastry chefs, confectioners, and ice–cream experts were all ready, and that everything was in good order.

The inaugural dinner of this new palace received nationwide coverage in the United States due to the following event. Until that day, no one had ever smoked in a dining room, even after dinner. But that night the guests decided to break this age-old custom. It created a scandal, and the next day all the major papers published an account entitled "The Scandal of the Ritz Hotel." Since then, custom has certainly changed; not only do people smoke after dinner, which is deplorable enough, but people even smoke during

151

meals. These meals where people smoke while eating should be baptized "dinner *à la nicotine.*" It is obvious that every dish from the appetizer to the dessert must have the same disagreeable taste.

During my six weeks in New York, the Ritz-Carlton Company, having just taken over the direction of the Grand Hotel in Pittsburgh, asked me to oversee the changes that needed to be made there: putting the kitchens in working order, hiring new chefs and kitchen staff, etc. I therefore went to Pittsburgh to get an idea of the situation and to take care of the most pressing renovations needed. This did not take long, and fifteen days after my visit, the chef and personnel I had recommended were able to start work.

* * *

My best memory of this period was being able to meet again with Sarah Bernhardt, that wonderful actress so beloved in America, and having the occasion to have lunch with her and her personal doctor several times at the Hôtel Marie-Antoinette, where she was staying.

During one of our luncheons I asked her the secret of her unfailing vitality, which everyone admired, and that she had managed to keep intact since her youth.

"My dear Escoffier," she smiled, "You are very nosy. There are secrets that a woman is born with, and that die with her."

I said, "Could you possibly be slightly selfish, to want to keep such secrets?"

"Yes and no," she replied. "When Nature has given you a certain gift, you must have the strength to say "I want..." and the courage to overcome all obstacles in the way! Let me invite you to lunch next Sunday, and I will tell you my little secrets then."

On the next Sunday I had just received a shipment of *pâté de foie gras* from Strasbourg, and while we were savoring this treasure of French delicacies, the wonderful woman shared her secret with me, a very simple one indeed: a very strong will, sustained by a glass of excellent champagne. Miss Bernhardt accompanied every meal with half a bottle of Moët et Chandon, and she told me that the sparkling wine from Champagne had the most marvelous effect on her.

That was on Christmas Eve. On December 27, I boarded the Cunard liner Lusitania, and I celebrated the end of 1910 and the beginning of the new year in the middle of the Atlantic. On January 4, 1911, I disembarked in Liverpool, and reached London that evening.

* * *

In the spring of 1911, after my return from the United States, I founded a magazine in London entitled *Le Carnet d'Epicure*. My aim, in publishing a French magazine abroad, was to contribute to the development of tourism in France, to bring attention to our beautiful landscapes, our historical monuments, our museums, and also to the best French products and how to prepare them.

I not only wrote of French cuisine, of our precious wines and fine liqueurs, but also of everything else pertaining to table service: silverware, crystal, glassware, porcelain table settings, lighting, flower arrangements, and the thousands of accessories that can complete a woman's style of dressing, the carefully kept secrets of our French fashion designers and milliners.

The magazine, as I conceived it, promised to have a brilliant future, with proper management. The low price of advertisements in *Le Carnet* enabled merchants, even those with low budgets, to advertise all kinds of products. *Le Carnet d'Epicure* was created in 1911, and circulation grew steadily until 1914, when the declaration of war between Germany and France forced me to stop publication. The last issue was dated August 5, 1914. Four years of war forced me to abandon this project, which I had created to help France.

* * *

I found among my papers the following article. It relates to the fire at the Carlton Hotel, a fire that put my life in danger.

Our readers have learned from the daily press about the disaster that has just taken place at the Carlton Hotel. On Wednesday, August 9, 1911, at 7:20 P.M., a fierce fire broke out in the kitchen elevators. At that very moment, our editor-in-chief had just taken his leave of Mr. Escoffier, who had gone up to his fifth-floor apartment in another elevator. The fire spread with frightening speed to the upper floors. A few minutes later, the fire had reached the roof of the building; the elevator which Mr. Escoffier had just used was engulfed in flames just after he left it. For half an hour all the witnesses on the scene were filled with anguish. It seemed impossible that Mr. Escoffier or any of the fifteen or twenty other persons trapped with him on floors above the fourth floor could possibly escape the furnace that was taking on more frightening proportions every minute.

Emergency rescue aid arrived from all parts of London. A huge crowd gathered in the main roads leading to the Carlton Hotel. Pall Mall, Haymarket, and even Trafalgar Square were packed with spectators, and the same frightening thoughts went through every mind in this crowd. At around 8:00 P.M. Mr. Escoffier and the other survivors were finally spotted coming down the fire escape of His Majesty's Theatre, the building adjoining the Carlton. The crowd applauded as they reached safety. In the sinister glow of the flames, this applause was so moving and tragic at the same time, that the scene was unforgettable.

The two top floors of the Carlton Hotel were entirely destroyed and the rest of the hotel was badly damaged by the flood of water poured into the building by fifty powerful pumps for over four hours.

At 1:00 A.M. we were finally able to cross the flooded grill room and gain access to the main dining hall, which was more or less untouched. There we found Mr. Escoffier surrounded by his staff. The material damage, amounting to over two million francs, did not faze Mr. Escoffier in the least.

"What do you expect?" he joked. "I have roasted so many millions of chickens in the twelve years I have been in this hotel that perhaps they wanted to take their revenge and roast me in turn! But they have only succeeded in singeing my feathers. I'll only have to replace my wardrobe."

Although all its rooms had been damaged, the Carlton was able to re-open its restaurant a few days later. Here is the first menu that was served after the fire.

Melon Fine Champagne
Consommé de Volaille Froid

• • •

Soles Coquelin

• • •

Selle d'Agneau aux Aubergines
Riz à l'Orientale

• • •

Grouse à l'Ecossaise
Salade Verte

• • •

Fonds d'Artichauts aux Fines Herbes

• • •

Soufflé Glacé aux Framboises
Friandises

The First *Dîner d'Epicure*

EVERY NEWSPAPER IN THE WORLD carried reports of our first Dîner d'Epicure.* Over and above our wildest expectations, it was the finest and most magnificent demonstration ever to take place in honor of French cuisine. That very evening, news of it was transmitted by telephone and telegraph to the four corners of the globe, and the world press printed articles the next morning in a burst of enthusiasm.

We will therefore limit ourselves to noting a few unpublished menus and giving our impression of the dinner held at the Hotel Cecil, transformed for that evening into the gastronomic center of the world.

We had counted on about a hundred guests, and considering that *Le Carnet d'Epicure* had barely existed for one year and that the *Ligue des*

---

* The Dîners d'Epicure were started by Escoffier in 1912, with members of his new gastronomic club *La Ligue des Gourmands*. A menu created by Escoffier was prepared and served simultaneously in fine restaurants of different towns and cities all over Europe to members of the Ligue and their friends. [ed.]

Gourmands was only three months old, we would have been presumptuous to expect otherwise. Yet there turned out to be 300 diners at the Hotel Cecil, and the same day, in thirty–seven other European cities, the exact same French meal was served to other members of our newborn *Ligue des Gourmands,* so that all over the world, at the same hour, there were over 4000 gourmets sitting down to the same meal.

The greatest warmth and cordiality reigned during this banquet, which was both grand and down to earth. I personally composed the menu; it was very warmly received by all the guests.

We had hardly begun the first course when the first telegram arrived. It came from Sarah Bernhardt. Our friend Bizeray stood on a chair to read it out loud.

> I am there with you all to take part in this beautiful and so very typical French celebration. My two hands stretch out to our great poet Richepin, to my dear friend Escoffier, and to you, Gringoire, who can create such beautiful poems to fruits and flowers; in fact to you all, friends of poetry and sensitive lovers of real life.

And then other telegrams arrived. Among them was one from Jean Richepin himself, which caused another enthusiastic round of applause when Bizeray stood on a table this time to read it.

> Long live the diners and the *dodineurs!** I am with them with all my heart, and join them to pay tribute to the truly great art that our French cuisine already is and must remain: a unique rose watered by the fine wines of France.

The cheers redoubled, and the journalists were no less enthusiastic, for they had not realized that two such undisputed stars of the world of art and poetry would participate with such fervor in our gastronomic celebration.

---

* For this epic dinner, Escoffier had revived an old recipe for *Dodine de Canard;* Richepin thus addressed the guests as "dodineurs," those who eat dodine. [ed.]

Here is the menu of this first Dîner d'Epicure:

Hors d'oeuvre Mignon
• • •
Petite Marmite Béarnaise
• • •
Truite Saumonée aux Crevettes Roses
• • •
Dodine de Canard au Chambertin
Nouilles Fraîches au Beurre Noisette
• • •
Agneau de Pauillac à la Bordelaise
Petits Pois Frais de Clamart
• • •
Poularde de France à la Gelée à la d'Orléans
• • •
Coeurs de Romaines aux Pommes d'Amour
Asperges d'Argenteuil Sauce Divine
• • •
Fraises Sarah Bernhardt
Mignardises
• • •
Café Mode Orientale
Les Plus Fines Liqueurs
• • •
Vins: Chablis Moutoune 1902
Chambertin Clos de Bèze 1887
Champagne Veuve Clicquot
Dry England 1900

Concerning the Word Dodine

A monk from Bergerac, Blaisius Ambrosius, is the author of a manu-script written in 1583 that can be found at the Château d'Ambelle, and that describes culinary pottery throughout the ages. He speaks of the *dodine*, a terrine in which food was cooked and that could be placed in ovens or buried in hot ashes. In the 1500s, a tile-maker of Perigueux, Pierre Loujou, earned quite a reputation manufacturing them. *Dodines* could resist the highest temperatures without cracking. They were made with sides several inches thick, and came in all sizes. They were used to cook boars' heads, for instance.

They must have existed in very large sizes because, as the story goes, some woodcutters of Verteillec, having caught a werewolf, enclosed it in a dodine to cook over a bonfire. They returned the next day to see if their werewolf was cooked, but when they took the *dodine* out of the ashes, the cover flew off and, to their stupefaction, the werewolf leaped out with such a frightening howl that their blood froze in their veins. Three of them dropped dead of fright and the others remained paralyzed for the rest of their lives. This is because, explains Blasius Ambrosius, the werewolf is none other than the Devil in disguise. No mere duck would ever have survived the *dodine*.

The *dodine* is not only the name of the cooking utensil but also of its cooked contents. The term *dodine* is first mentioned in the *Viandier* of Taillevant, the chef of French King Charles V, but it no doubt already existed for ages. All cookbooks dating before the seventeenth century contain the same recipes as the *Viandier*, a manuscript written in 1380. The term *dodine* was not only reserved for duck; it applied to all birds, fowl, and game. Red *dodine* was made with Suresne wine and white *dodine* was based on milk.

Although the *dodine rouge* (red dodine) was really merely a salmi, I feel it would be of interest to revive this pleasing name for use in our menus, even if the old recipes are only of documentary value today. Despite the fact that French cuisine has evolved since the time of Pierre Pidoux, we owe it to them to respect these cooks of another school, since our own culinary art stems from their experiments, even if they may seem rudimentary to us today.

Dodine au Chambertin

Choose a large fattened Rouen duck and clean it carefully; empty it, put aside the liver and season the insides with salt, pepper, and a few drops of excellent Armagnac. Truss the bird; roast it until cooked rare, and let it cool; remove the 2 breasts and keep them warm in a covered platter. Make sure to place the breasts skin side down; this is important in order to save all the juice found in the flesh. Remove the tail (or "parson's nose") completely and discard. Cut off the thighs (they will not be used in the *dodine*, but can be used in another dish). Crush the rest of the duck carcass with a pestle.

For each duck, mix into a casserole the following ingredients: a large glass of Chambertin wine (not too old), 2 small glasses of cognac, 2 minced shallots, a pinch of grated nutmeg, half a laurel leaf, and a pinch of pepper. Boil for several minutes; add the crushed carcass and 1/3 liter of demi-glace sauce thickened with a small amount of brown veal stock. Boil for 12–15 minutes and then rub the mixture vigorously through a fine sieve. Replace the sauce in the casserole, boil for 1 minute, and keep hot without boiling. Put a few knobs of butter on the top of the sauce to prevent the formation of a skin.

Take the duck's liver, add 2 other duck livers if possible (or else some carefully cleaned chicken livers), season them with salt and pepper, sauté them in hot butter over a high flame, and, as soon as they are sealed, pass them through a fine sieve. Mix the purée thus obtained into the warm sauce.

Separately, prepare a *ragoût* consisting of sliced truffle, minced *cèpe* (edible boletus) sautéed in butter, braised cockscombs, and cock kidneys fried in butter. Add the warm sauce to this *ragoût*.

To serve: In a warmed porcelain platter (slightly hollow and oval) with a cover, place the duck breasts cut into 3 or 4 slices according to size, and add the flavorful *ragoût*, heated through. During the *foie gras* season, one can add a slice of *foie gras* sautéed in butter for each guest. Cover the platter and serve immediately.

Fraises à la Sarah Bernhardt
(SERVES 8-10)

Choose 3–4 pounds of fresh greenhouse strawberries and remove their stems. Put 2/3 of the nicest ones in an enameled tureen, sprinkle them with powdered sugar, add 5–6 glasses of Vieille Cure, and place the tureen on ice. Pass the rest of the strawberries through a fine sieve, mix 250 grams of sugar into the resulting purée, and add it to the rest of the strawberries. Separately, use preserves of pineapple to prepare a fruit pulp as follows: with one fork hold the pineapple in place, and with another fork tear the fruit into a pulp. Sprinkle with 250 grams of sugar and keep on ice. In advance, prepare 1 1/2 liters of vanilla ice cream and 3/4 liters of whipped cream Chantilly.

To serve: Take a crystal bowl of the necessary size, fill the bottom with vanilla ice cream, and place the whole strawberries on top. Mix the strawberry purée into the whipped cream Chantilly. Cover the strawberries with the pineapple pulp and then add the whipped cream *à la fraise*. The mixture of the last 2 ingredients should be such as to give the illusion of a beautiful sunset. Throw a lace of spun sugar over this delicious dessert to complete the presentation.

Aboard the *Imperator*
with Kaiser Wilhelm II

1913

IN THE YEAR 1913, a great banquet was held on the liner *Imperator*, a veritable floating city that had just been built to link Hamburg and New York. The Kaiser, showing great interest in the Hamburg America Company, decided to spend a few days on board prior to its maiden transatlantic crossing.

The Carlton had taken over the management of the restaurant, just as they had for the Amerika and the Kaiserin Augusta Victoria, and I was asked to personally manage the restaurant for this event.

I arrived on board the Imperator on Saturday, July 7, 1913, to make the first preparations for the royal reception. The 110 guests arrived two days later. Among them were the most famous names of German aristocracy.

The Emperor arrived with his court on Tuesday, July 10, at 10:00 A.M. The *Imperator* immediately raised anchor in the direction of the Helgoland Islands. His Majesty lunched at 1:00 P.M. with his guests, and dinner was planned for 8:00 P.M. After dinner, the Emperor and his guests watched a motion picture. Several scenes amused them greatly, especially one involving lobster fishing, with a lovely French actress in the leading role. The highlight of the evening was another film explaining the submarine maneuvers of the French fleet in Tunis, and that closed the entertainment for the evening.

This film left a deep impression on me. I thought it was quite out of place under the circumstances. Rumors of war were already abounding, and the film could only be of service to Germany and compromise the security of France. I was troubled by this memory for a long time afterwards.

The Kaiser sent me a message that he wished to see me the next morning after breakfast. The liner continued sailing all night and at 8:00 A.M. it landed in Cuxhaven.

It was about 10:00 A.M. when His Majesty left the restaurant and came down to the Palm Room. He shook my hand and told me how much he appreciated the comfort he had found on board, and how pleased he had been to spend as quiet a night on board as he might have in his own palace. He thanked me for having come especially from London to take care of the restaurant during his stay on board.

I thanked him for the sympathy he had shown me and asked him for news of Her Majesty's health and that of all of his family. He told me that all of his family were in good health, and thanked me for my concern.

Then I said to him, "Your Majesty, I hope that your health will enable you to reign for a long time, and I pray that before the end of your reign, we will see the time when the greatest of all humanitarian acts will have been accomplished: the reconciliation of Germany and France."

The Emperor assured me that it was also his greatest desire, and that he did everything to work to that purpose, but that unfortunately it was often difficult and rare to see one's best intentions correctly interpreted.

I remarked that some newspapers seemed to me to be animated by regrettable sentiments.

"Indeed," he replied, "the press, or rather some parts of the press, is not favorable to good ideas, but despite that, I have great hopes of seeing my desires realized, and I pray for it with all my heart, for the greater welfare of all mankind."

"I hope, Your Majesty, that both sides will show their good will, and that you will have the joy of seeing the reconciliation of these two great countries, which would be the crowning achievement of your reign and mean the good fortune of all the peoples of Europe."

Hardly one year after this brilliant reception, Germany declared war on France. On November 1, 1914, my son Daniel, lieutenant in the 363rd Alpine Regiment, was hit full in the face by a Prussian bullet and died instantly, leaving his four children for me to bring up.

* * *

Here is the menu I had composed for the reception on the *Imperator*:

Hors d'oeuvre à la Russe
Melon Cantaloup

• • •

Consommé Froid Madrilène
Velouté Parmentier

• • •

Timbale de Homard Impérator
Mousse de Jambon au Madère
Epinards Nouveau

• • •

Selle de Veau Orloff
Pointes d'Asperges au Beurre

• • •

Dodine de Canard en Gelée
Terrine de Poulet à l'Estragon

• • •

Salade de Fruits à la Japonaise
Aubergines à l'Orientale

• • •

Soufflé Glacé Framboisé
Biscuit au Kirsch

• • •

Pâtisserie Française
Fruits
Café Liqueurs

• • •

Vins:
Georges Goulet Extra Dry
Clicquot Rosé
Zeltinger Schoessberg
Château Giscourt, 1907

The War, Seen from London

1914–1918

On the night Germany invaded Belgium in August 1914, Lloyd George and Winston Churchill were dining at the Carlton. Ho Chi Minh, the future communist leader of North Vietnam, was working in Escoffier's kitchen preparing vegetables.

LIKE A STORM THAT APPEARS out of clear skies, in August 1914, without warning, Germany invaded the small and valiant country of Belgium, and we were immediately thrown into a state of war.

Germany, of course, announced that this would be a very short war due to the strength of their troops and their surprise attack. They thought that they were going to take over Paris within a few weeks and that France, therefore, would have to lay down her arms and sign a peace treaty.

They had not taken into account the resistance of Belgium and the landing of the British troops. They had also forgotten that the French still had guts. The Battle of the Marne taught them that their hopes were premature.

In London, the food situation quickly became worrying. The population was afraid to run short and decided to stock up on provisions. Every day greater and greater crowds invaded the grocery stores.

During this time the British government, reacting with great prudence and resolution, took the measures needed to sustain its army and its people. Provisions were rationed to prevent waste. Twice a week, everyone had to give up meat and potatoes.

To buy meat or poultry in a butcher shop, one had to produce a coupon. Venison, luckily, was exempt from coupons; this was a great boon to restaurants.

As such, at the Carlton, eggs with minced venison soon became a gastronomic delight. In this time of scarcity, venison frequently meant chewy meat from old deer; it often had to be braised to be edible. With the addition of rice, one might turn it into a decent *moussaka*. However, deer meat stewed in *daube à la provençale*, accompanied by noodles and especially by a chestnut purée, turned out to be an excellent dish.

We could vary our menus with products like eggs, fish, giblets, and bacon, which were not rationed. The government fixed such high prices for certain fish, such as sole and salmon, that they were difficult to come by. I needed thirty or forty salmon per week, and could hardly get two from my supplier. I finally made direct contact with fishermen from Scotland and Ireland, and they were able to give me total satisfaction.

One fish that came to my rescue during this period was the small lemon sole. I found that it could advantageously replace regular sole in many ways. One simply needed to separate the fillets, clean them, salt them lightly, flour them, dip them in beaten egg, and then roll them in breadcrumbs. As there was no real butter, I cooked them in cocoa butter instead. I also always carefully kept a little stock of chicken grease for emergencies. These breaded fillets of lemon sole, sautéed in a *poêle*, were served on a bed of macaroni *à la Napolitaine*, and was a very successful dish.

It is the duty of a *chef de cuisine* never to be caught unawares. As we know, when fresh fish from the morning tide failed to be delivered, France's great chef Vatel lost his senses and threw himself on his sword to save his professional honor. Once, during a culinary exhibit in Tours, a gentleman approached me and asked, "What would you have done, sir, in Vatel's place?"

*François Vatel
(1635–1671) was a
famous seventeenth-
century chef first
employed as steward
by the financier
Fouquet, and later
attached to the noble
house of Chantilly.
In April 1671, the
prince of Condé
entrusted him with
the task of organiz-
ing a fête in honor of
Louis XIV, with
3,000 guests. In the
course of the supper
following a hunting
party, several tables
lacked roast meat
because a number of
unexpected guests
turned up. Later, the
planned fireworks
display was spoiled
by a cloudy sky.
Learning at dawn on
the following day
that only two loads
of the fresh fish
ordered for the meals
of the day had
arrived from the
coast, Vatel gave
way to despair,
declaring, "I shall
not survive this dis-
grace." He shut him-
self in his room and
ran his sword
through his body,
just as the fish carts
were entering the
castle gates.*

Rather surprised, I answered, "Surely, I would never have thrown myself on a sword for a question of tide. I would have replaced the fillets of sole with the flesh of young chickens, and I bet even the most exacting gourmet would never have noticed the difference!"

"But how can you make fillets of sole out of chicken?" he exclaimed. "I can't understand it!"

"Very well, I'll give you the recipe. You choose very young chickens, and after having cleaned them, crush up their flesh with a pestle. Then add one quarter the volume of white bread lightly moistened with very fresh cream, a little salt, and one egg white for each two chickens. Mix this together again for several minutes, pass the mixture through a fine sieve, and place the resulting purée on a floured surface. Divide it into parts (about fifty or sixty grams each), roll them into cigar shapes, and flatten them slightly with a knife in order to give them the aspect of a fillet of sole. Dip them in beaten egg and then in very fine bread crumbs. Tap the fillets with the flat of a knife blade lightly so that the bread crumbs stick to the egg. Ten minutes before serving, cook the fillets in clarified butter until they are golden brown on both sides. Serve them immediately on a hot platter and cover them with an excellent anchovy butter, slightly spiced with paprika. To make the dish even more regal, one could add a garnish of thin slices of fresh truffle, slightly heated in melted butter and with a few teaspoons of chicken grease. These delicious chicken fillets could be presented under the name *Filets de Sole Monseigneur*."

* * *

Although during all this wartime period, supply problems were my principal worry, I also had another serious preoccupation. I had to help the families of my staff members that had been called to the French front, who were all facing serious difficulties. To do so, I created a support committee and solicited numerous donations, thanks to which many problems were solved. Every week, we shared a certain sum of money among fifty women and seventy children. At the end of the war, a total sum of 75,000 francs had been distributed. I had personally known the most humble sufferings, and could not do otherwise than try to find a solution to those of others. At the

Savoy and the Carlton, for instance, I was always overstaffed by one or two workers in order to help the unemployment problem. As for those of my staff that had been called to the front, I took every measure necessary to make sure that they would find work again in our kitchens at the end of the war.

* * *

The unforgettable day of November 11, 1918, came to deliver the population from the terrible nightmare that they had endured with such courage for four long years.

The English, who normally have a very calm temperament, were overtaken by a delirious joy when they heard the good news, and perfect strangers could be seen kissing each other in the street. They had had the same reaction when the peace treaty ending the Boer War was signed. I have kept a warm memory of these moments that were full of joy and hope. I was able to appreciate both the normal calm of these people and the spontaneity that enabled them to celebrate.

The armistice was announced at 11:00 A.M., and the restaurant was immediately swamped with calls from our regular patrons, who wanted to reserve tables to celebrate the end of these terrible years. At 1:00 P.M. every single table was already reserved for dinner. And I had to prepare 712 meals!

At the time, food restrictions were most severe, especially for meat. On that day I had only six legs of lamb, two small veal haunches, fifteen kilograms of fresh pork, and ten chickens. I took all of this meat and put it through the mincer. I added twenty kilograms of canned *pâté de foie gras* that I had left over from before the war, some minced truffle, and about ten kilograms of bread watered down with sterilized cream. I then cooked this mixture as small *noisettes* that were, frankly, very much appreciated. I called my dish *Mignonnettes d'Agneau Sainte–Alliance*.

Never lose your head, even when faced with great difficulty. That must be the motto of every *chef de cuisine*.

Here is the menu of the dinner that was served at the Carlton Hotel in London on the occasion of the Armistice, November 11, 1918 (718 covers):

1918: "Hunger does not breed reform; it breeds madness," said U.S. President Wilson in an Armistice Day address to Congress.

Diner au Champagne

Consommé du Père la Victoire
Velouté Renaissance

• • •

Mousseline de Homard à l'Américaine
Riz à l'Indienne

• • •

Petits Pâtés de Volaille à la Bruxelloise

• • •

Mignonnettes d'Agneau Sainte–Alliance
Petits Pois à l'Anglaise
Pommes de Terre Canadiennes

• • •

Faisan en Cocotte Périgourdine
Salade des Capucins

• • •

Coeurs de Céleri à l'Italienne

• • •

Les Bombes de Réjouissance
Symbole de la Paix

• • •

Les Douces Dragées de Verdun Libératrices
Friandises

• • •

Liqueurs de France Café Mode Orientale
Fine Champagne, 1865
Vieille Chartreuse du Couvent

* * *

The Légion d'Honneur medals were established on May 19, 1802, by Napoléon Bonaparte to recognize and reward excellence and achievement in every sphere.

On November 11, 1919, the anniversary of the day when peace was signed, I had one of the most rewarding days of my professional life. On that day, Mr. Poincaré, President of the French Republic, gave a reception at the Palace of St. James for the French colony living in London. I had no idea that I was on the list of people who were to receive a token of appreciation from the French government during the President's trip in this great city. I was astonished to hear my name pronounced, and to receive from the President's hand the medal of *Chevalier de la Legion d'Honneur.** I was very

* Knight of the Legion of Honor. [ed.]

proud of this distinction and told M. Poincaré how happy it made me, thanking him for the honor that he had bestowed on me by presenting it to me himself. This is a memory that will always remain engraved in my heart.

Advice to Professionals
L'Aide Mémoire Culinaire

Right after the war, I published *L'Aide Mémoire Culinaire*, intended for professionals in culinary art, a book that tried to take into account all the changes that circumstances have dictated in the business.

For instance, it is absolutely necessary that waiters be able to answer the questions of any customer wanting to know the content of any dish, without having to ask somebody in the kitchen. Therefore, they need precise information put forth concisely, and that was one of the purposes of my publication.

The client also wants to know which wines best accompany which dishes. I will later address the importance of the serving of wine.

In this post-war period, many changes took place, and these changes will probably continue to amplify as the years go by. In the years to come our war-torn countries will have to restabilize their finances, and enormous sacrifices will have to be made by everyone to accomplish this. The luxurious and prodigious lifestyle that we knew will die, leaving in its wake a period when thrift will be absolutely necessary, as will a return to simplicity. But this simplicity can be one of good taste, excluding neither the savory perfection of our cuisine nor the correct elegance of our service.

Because I have an eye on the future, I thought it was necessary to break with the old traditions of French cuisine that the modern world has rendered obsolete, while still keeping in mind the high standards of quality that have made it a universal art. I therefore revised and simplified many of my old recipes, adapted them to present circumstances, eliminated many that were not of great interest, and kept those that were of obvious importance and could be of use every day. This kind of methodic selection was necessary to eliminate mundane repetition.

I have spent fifty-six years in the kitchens of large restaurants and I can therefore see the deficiencies that currently exist in their various departments, and the problems that need to be addressed.

We have excellent cooks in France, and we also have, and have always had, excellent *maîtres d'hôtel* who know their profession inside and out. They are the masters of *à la carte* service and all foreigners coming to our restaurants are unanimous in recognizing their tact and their polite and dignified kindness. If the star of their reputation has been slightly shadowed by a passing cloud, it is due to the sudden and extraordinary expansion of the number of restaurants in France. Young men were so rapidly trained to be *maîtres d'hôtel* that many of them found themselves in a position requiring a competence that they had not had the time to acquire.

I am afraid this situation may worsen, due to the war, or at least until new personnel can be found, men that have been trained in the schools we hope will be created, or at least have been trained by a good existing *maître d'hôtel*.

Wine Service

In an era when all sorts of preoccupations shorten the time that was once spent eating, it is not surprising that profound changes have come to the culinary world.

Without going as far back as the beginning of the last century, everyone knows that under the Second Empire and until 1890, meals were opulent and required a great deal of service, for food as well as for wines, and that the dishes served were almost as numerous as during the First Empire and the Restoration period (except for the *à la russe* service, where dishes are presented one after the other, which replaced service *à la française*, where all dishes of the same course are placed on the table together).

Current fashion and habits are such that one can only spend one hour, or an hour and a half, at any single meal.

For the last thirty years, even the most substantial menus have generally been made up of only one or two soups, an *hors d'oeuvre* (hot or cold), a fish, two entrées, a roast, a cold meat, a salad, one or two accompanying vegetables, two hot or cold sweets, and various desserts.

In the old days, depending on the importance of the host and the number of his invited guests, the expected menu consisted of an incredible number of dishes that we can hardly imagine today; if we examine the culinary literature of the eighteenth century and the beginning of the nineteenth century, we find menus that had between thirty and sixty dishes, not to mention the desserts, which were often just as numerous.

But in none of this literature can we find the names of the wines that were served, nor the order they were served in.

At the end of Viard's *Cuisinier Royal*, we find a note on wine service by Mr. Pierhugue, the King's wine waiter, but no mention is made of the order in which wines were served during the course of a meal.

Viard was a celebrated nineteenth-century French chef, author of a collection of recipes entitled Le Cuisinier Impérial *(1806), which in 1817 was published as* Le Cuisinier Royal, *with a supplementary chapter on wines. It was a basic reference book for chefs throughout the nineteenth century.*

It seems that the rule, fifty years ago, in wine service was the following:

- Madeira or Sherry, or a similar wine, after soup, melon, or *hors d'oeuvre.*

- White wine, dry, demi-sec, or sweet (Chablis, Meursault, Pouilly, Graves, Sauternes, Rhine, Moselle) with oysters or fish.

- To quench thirst, ordinary table wine during the entire meal.

- For entrées: a high quality Bordeaux.

- To accompany the roast: a first vintage Burgundy.

- To accompany sweet desserts: Champagne, or sometimes Port or wine from Haut-Sauternes.

This is still the rule today for formal meals, and a rational one, taking into account that light wines must be served with delicate dishes and more robust ones with seasoned dishes.

In the last few years, a more reasonable attitude has modified the service of wine.

We have recognized that starting a meal with such strong wines as Madeira, Sherry, and or Haut-Sauternes did not help the appreciation of the other wines that would be served during the meal, and that the mixture of a great variety of wines in one meal tended to affect both the head and the stomach.

Whatever wines are to be served during the meal, it is best to start with light wines, and then progressively turn to more robust ones. But wine service does not only consist of the order in which they are presented.

To display the quality of the wine and to produce the satisfaction desired, the bottles must be taken out of the cellar the day before they are meant to be served, if possible, and carried with great care and placed upright in the pantry or dining room so that they can reach room temperature. One hour before they are to be served, they should be uncorked and the wine should be decanted.

Decanting a wine is an extremely delicate operation that true gourmets prefer to take on themselves rather than let allow amateurs to try their hand at it. It doesn't mean, as so often happens, simply pouring the wine into a pitcher, but truly being able to separate the liquid from its sediment by a careful movement that prevents the deposit from mixing in with the wine itself. For aged red wines, decanting is essential. Not only does it enable the wine to breathe, but it also eliminates the cloudiness that the sediment would cause, and gives the wine all of its transparency and brilliance.

If for any reason it is not possible to decant a wine, it is best to keep the bottle in a horizontal position, lay it in a special wine basket, uncork it gently, wipe the neck clean, and pour the wine without unduly lifting up the basket.

If white wines must be decanted for the beauty of the table service, this should be done only a few minutes before serving in order to avoid the cloudiness caused by the wine's oxidizing in contact with the air.

Dry or regular wine can be served during the meal and should precede the Bordeaux or Burgundy that will be offered with the cheese.

I cannot but strongly criticize those *maîtres d'hôtel* who serve wine and actually lift up the bottle in between each glass poured, because it is obvious that the sediment is stirred at each move, and the wine is therefore muddied and loses its taste.

Many people believe that for cooking they can use wines that are of poor quality or have even turned. They think that even so these wines are good enough for any stew. This is the kind of erroneous thinking that we must fight against. Without necessarily being fine vintage of Burgundy or Bordeaux, cooking wines must be natural, robust, and good tasting. This is the only way to turn out an excellent dish.

And then, I would like to protest against the current use of the names of French wines to sell products that do not come from our country. In the last few years, I have seen wines for sale in England labeled Burgundy wine or wine from Bourgogne that are actually made in Australia, California, or sometimes even London itself, and that can in no way compare either in aroma, or in the richness of *bouquet*, or in beneficial effects, to our natural wine from Bourgogne. Englishmen of the highest class are connoisseurs too fine to be fooled by these wines, but in many restaurants they are served as real Burgundy wine. It is really regrettable that this kind of confusion is tolerated, both for the reputation of our wines, and for the English people themselves, because, without paying a higher price, they could offer themselves infinitely superior wines than those they buy under the so-called label of Bourgogne—from Australia or California!

When traveling through Burgundy in 1906, I visited the cellars of the Abbaye de Lieu-Dieu and spoke about this problem with its owner, Mrs. Vermelen de Villiers, while she was showing me around her property. She told me that during the reign of Louis XV, the nuns of this abbey had won a lawsuit at Dijon against a wine merchant from Nuit who sold his wine as coming from Lieu–Dieu.

The Success of
Our Food Products Abroad

DESPITE COMPETITION FROM other countries, French food products, both fresh and preserved, have always found a good market throughout the world. The reason for this popularity is not only to be found in the care we take in our products; it is also due to the fact that our cooks abroad are legion. These traveling salesmen in high white toques are our best agents, as they keep up the tradition of serving French products even when they are far from home. And by inventing new culinary creations, they often create new openings for French products.

Here are some examples to prove it:

Since I created *Pêche Melba*, which now enjoys world wide renown, demand for tender peaches, both fresh and preserved whole, has increased considerably. To ensure the high quality of such peaches, the fruit must not be too fragile. Montreuil peaches were excellent, but in recent years that quality of peach became difficult to find. I noticed that in the Rhône valley there grew a peach that was very similar to the Montreuil peach. I tested it and was very happy with the results. The next year, in 1911, 15,000 of these peaches were canned. The year after, 30,000 peaches were canned, and the third year the figure had reached 60,000. The producer was planning to can 100,000 of these peaches when the war broke out. This kind of incontestable success would never had existed without the creation of *Pêche Melba.*

The French truffle has also enjoyed increasing popularity because of our cooks. Current sales reach several million francs and are a great source of income for the Périgord, the Vaucluse, and the Dauphiné regions.

In London I never used any fresh butter other than that of the Brétel brothers, especially that marked in blue, first quality butter from Brittany and Normandy. The 150 pounds of butter I used every day amounted to 4,500 pounds a month, quite an impressive volume for just one chef!

The Rouen duck, another good example, was practically unknown in England in the 1880s. No London tradesman had ever heard of it. Today, however, one can find Rouen duck in any reputable food store. It is almost more popular in London than in Paris. What contributed enormously to its popularity was the many ways it could be cooked, especially *Canard en chemise*; the word *chemise** might be shocking to the English, but it certainly helped to extend the popularity of the Rouen duck!

Here is a story concerning green asparagus. When the aged Baron de Rothschild came to eat at the Grand Hôtel in Monte Carlo, he always asked for green asparagus. To satisfy him, we had to choose the biggest asparagus from our bunches of white asparagus tips. When I was at the Savoy in later years, I noticed that the English also preferred green asparagus to white. I therefore sent to France for big green tips, and they were so successful that demand soon exceeded supply, and within a few days their price simply doubled.

Faced with the producer's asking price, I had to find a competitor to keep the cost down. One Sunday morning, I met with some asparagus farmers in a café in Mérindol, a village close to Lauris in the region of the Vaucluse. "Gentlemen," I told them, "You produce some very fine asparagus, but it gives you great trouble and very little financial reward to do it. I live in London and take care of the kitchens of a very big hotel. And the English prefer green

---

* Shirt or vest, often meant as undergarment. Food prepared *en chemise* is wrapped in pastry or coated with sauce or aspic. [ed.]

asparagus. Would it interest you to produce them for me? I guarantee you that it would be well worth your while."

All of these good men were rather taken aback, and told me that to grow green asparagus would force them to change their farming system, and that they could hardly see their way clear to doing that. Then a young man, in his twenties, stood up and said, "Why not? Growing alongside our big asparagus, we have a quantity of small ones that we sell for less than nothing. If we let these sprout, the part that reaches the light will turn green and make green asparagus."

Everyone realized the impact of this idea, and from that day on, Lauris exported green asparagus to England. The vegetable was even more successful than I had predicted. In London, everyone asked for green Lauris asparagus instead of the white variety. And I never received even one bunch of asparagus as a gift from a producer, although my advice must have made rich men out of several of them!

Tomatoes were thought to be poisonous until the eighteenth century, and they did not reach Paris markets until around 1830. In the United States, the tomato seems to have been eaten during most of the nineteenth centruy, but in the latter part the vegetable was shunned because it was thought to cause cancer.

Crushed tomato appeared on the market around 1892. But the idea of producing it came in 1874–75, when I was chef at Le Petit Moulin Rouge. At the time it was the custom to put tomato purée in Champagne bottles and then sterilize them. This purée could only be used for tomato sauce. I thought the taste could be improved, and carried out tests that were entirely satisfactory. I understood that it would be beneficial to our food industry to advertise this product and spoke of it to several manufacturers, but no one was interested in the idea. Fifteen years later I was able to convince a fruit and vegetable canning factory to produce 2,000 cans of crushed tomato that were immediately sent to the Savoy. They were very much appreciated, and canned tomato sauce was launched. Its popularity was such that in the next year, 60,000 kilos of canned crushed tomatoes were produced. Later, the rate of production increased even more, spreading to Italy and America. Today millions of cans of tomato sauce are sold. This was due to my tenacity and the confidence that I always had in the success this product. And I had no other motivation than a desire to be useful.

I also took an interest in the production of the special sauces and canned pickles that the English like so much. During the war I had to give up the shares I had in the company that manufactured them according to my recipes, but they are still sold with a label carrying my name.

An Active Retirement

In May 1920, tired out by too much work during the four years of war, I decided to retire to enjoy what rest I could find. In July, I left the Carlton Hotel, leaving behind twenty years of memories of working at this establishment and of all the influential people I had met there. I was most pleased by the warmth and friendship of the directors and administrators of the hotel, and the kindness of the staff, which numbered over 400.

I therefore left England, a country to which I had become very attached, and my many friends, and returned home to my family in Monte Carlo to take advantage of the invigorating Riviera sunshine.

But as I was used to a very active life, after a few months of rest I soon became bored. I spent my time writing memoirs, articles, and recipes, aiming to maintain the excellent reputation of our French cuisine and fine wines.

I also participated in various culinary exhibitions. In 1911, before the war, I had been asked to preside at the one held in Frankfurt, an honor that was bestowed on me as a representative of every French chef. I was again told of the high esteem in which Wilhelm II held me, and someone added, "If an Escoffier existed in Germany, all the menus of the world would be written in French!" It is true that art transcends all borders, but for the time being, and for a long time to come, I hope, France stands in first place in the realm of culinary art.

In 1923, during the culinary exhibition in Copenhagen, I was honored with an invitation to meet the royal family of Denmark. I was surprised and very touched when they presented me with the Daneborg Cross, the first to be awarded to an artist. A great banquet was held on this occasion, under the direction of a French chef, and I participated by creating *soufflé Princesse Renée*, decorated in red and white to symbolize the national colors of Denmark.

In 1926 I was asked to preside over the jury of the culinary exhibition held in Grenoble. Every reputable restaurant and hotel in town and the surrounding region participated in this demonstration. I was extremely satisfied to see that the dishes were executed with great artistry, and that the warm congratulations to their creators were very much deserved. It reinforced my conviction that today's cooks are fully capable of maintaining the fine traditions of a glorious past.

The Zurich international culinary exhibition took place in 1930. I was pleasantly surprised to find out that the great hall in which the exhibition took place had been baptized "Boulevard Escoffier." I was invited to visit the huge and very modern factory that manufactures Maggi products, situated on the outskirts of Zurich. Most of the vegetables used in manufacturing Maggi soups were cultivated in huge fields around the factory. I was amazed at the speed with which the soups were prepared, in the best sanitary conditions.

In 1926, as a guest of the Cunard Line of London, I went to the United States for the third time, aboard their liner Berengaria. This was the old Hamburg–Amerika flagship *Imperator*; it had been renamed and given to

England by Germany at the end of the war to replace the *Lusitania* sunk by German submarines.

My voyage on the former *Imperator* awoke many conflicting memories in me, both those of the brilliant banquet I had prepared in honor of Wilhelm II in 1913, and those of the dark days that followed in 1914–18 during the first World War.

In New York I stayed at the Ambassador Hotel, and was very touched by the enthusiastic welcome that the entire kitchen staff gave me. I was especially pleased to recognize many who had worked under my orders at the Savoy, at the Carlton, and even in Monte Carlo.

One evening at the Carlton in New York, a dinner was held that brought together all the French and American culinary societies. Many young apprentice chefs were present as well. I reminded them that our profession is a crucial one, as everyone has to eat. It fills a real need, and there is no danger that it will disappear. I exhorted them to unite their efforts and bring all of their good will to bear so that *haute cuisine* would keep its excellent reputation. It is due to their skills and their constant efforts that they merit the title of *cuisinier* and not just cook. A *cuisinier* is a man who is capable of bringing together professional skill, personal initiative, and great experience in his craft. A cook is too often a man who has just one tool: a can opener!

At the end of this banquet, the president, Mr. Scotto, presented me with a magnificent gold plaque inscribed with two laurel wreaths around the *Légion d'Honneur*.

In 1930 I once again visited the land of the dollar. The owner of a new palace, the Hotel Pierre, asked me to preside over the banquet held for the opening of the hotel on October 16, 1930. I made the trip from Paris to New York in seven days on the liner *Paris*, and all my friends and colleagues were waiting for me when I disembarked.

I had a very heavy schedule during this trip. I was invited to a dinner held in my honor nearly every night. But the most memorable of all of them was the one where we celebrated my eighty-fifth birthday in the reception rooms of the Hotel Pierre, on October 28, 1930. Here is the menu that was served:

Escoffier's 1926 and 1930 trips to the United States took place during the Prohibition period, 1920–1933. While the Eighteenth Amendment did not succeed in eliminating drinking, it did set back the development of haute cuisine because people were not eager to dine in dry restaurants, no matter how exceptional the food.

Cold Appetizers:

Fantaisies Parisiennes
Barquerolles Strasbourgeoise
Oeufs à la Crème d'Anchois

Hot Appetizers:

Rissoles au Parmesan
Petits Pâtés Chauds à la Provençale
Tartelettes Forestières
Pommes d'Amour aux Huîtres Pimentées
Velouté à l'Orientale

Suprême de Sole Isaline

• • •

Poulet Nouveau Valentinois
Petits Pois à la Française
Salade Châtelaine

• • •

Symbole de la Vertu
Mignardises

• • •

Café Ancienne Mode
Liqueurs

Despite my eighty-five years of age, I had no problem with these daily banquets. I was in excellent shape when I left New York on the *Aquitania* at the end of October. I disembarked at Liverpool, stayed two days in London to see old friends, and then returned to Paris. The day after my arrival, during a luncheon at the Lucas restaurant, on the place de la Madeleine, that was organized by the Société Mutuelle des Cuisiniers Français, I had the pleasure of giving the president of this association ten thousand francs for culinary school, a sum that resulted from gifts from various private donors and organizations in America. At the same time I was able to give them some good news: in New York I had obtained permission for more French chefs to work on English and American liners.

I believe I can say that I did my best to fulfill my role as ambassador for French cuisine.

In March 1928 I was awarded the rank of *Officier de la Légion d'Honneur*. I was the first chef to receive this mark of distinction as a reward for many long years of labor in the service of French cuisine. But I knew that this honor would be reflected on all members of our profession. A great banquet was held on this occasion in the Hotel du Palais d'Orsay. It was presided over by Edouard Herriot, who was at the time Minister of Public Instruction and Fine Arts. All members of the elite Parisian high society were present, as well as influential personalities in the world of hotels, restaurants, and the press. There were 350 guests in all.

Many speeches were made. They all bore witness to the high esteem and unanimous friendship that everyone held for me. I must say that my emotions and my pride were very strong.

I have often been asked why I thought French chefs were superior to those from other countries. The answer seems simple enough to me. One only needs to understand that the French soil has the privilege to naturally and abundantly produce the best vegetables, the best fruits, and the best wines that exist in the world. France also has the best poultry, the most tender meat, and the most varied and delicate kinds of game. France's shores yield the finest kinds of fish and shellfish. It is therefore only natural that Frenchmen have become both gourmets and fine chefs.

But for a population to enjoy fine cuisine, it is also important that they should have had a long heritage of a courteous style of living that stresses the importance of a good meal celebrated among friends, and that there should be a strong domestic tradition whereby all the secrets of fine cooking are transmitted from mother to daughter. In the reputation of our French cuisine I see proof of our degree of civilization.

There is probably not one village in France where the healthy traditions of the local cuisine have not been religiously preserved. Each region is a treasure house of old recipes. Each village has its succulent traditional dish, prepared the same way for the last few centuries, and impossible to duplicate elsewhere.

One needs only to make a rapid tour of France to prove the point. Strasbourg competes with Toulouse to make the best *pâté de foie gras*. Angoulême and Périgueux compete over the best partridge *pâtés*. Bresse produces the finest chicken; Le Mans and La Flèche the best capon; the Périgord the best truffle–stuffed turkey. Nérac and Cahors produce fine terrines; Sarlat has its scarlet–legged partridge; Lyon makes excellent *cervelat* sausage. Arles is famous for its salami; Troyes produces fine small tongue, *andouilles* (chitterling sausage), and its inimitable pork brawn; the Dauphiné has rock partridge; Marennes, Cancale, and Etretat are famous for oysters; Strasbourg has carp and freshwater crayfish; Marseilles has fresh and marinated tuna fish; Rouen produces duckling and excellent jams; Dijon, Châlons, and Reims are famous for mustard; Aix-en-Provence, Grasse, and Nice produce the best olive oil and candied fruit; Verdun produces *dragées* (sugared almonds); Metz has figs and plums; Chartres offers its *guignards* and fowl *pâtés*; Pithiviers serves the skylark *en croûte*; Granville, marinated oysters; Alençon, fatted geese; Niort has its angelica; Orléans has its vinegar; Cognac has its brandy; Bordeaux has its anisette; Sète has its rose oil; Montpellier has its *crème moka*; Brignoles has its prunes; Roquevaire has admirable *panses*; Ollioules has fine figs; Agen has its plums *du Roi*; Tours has its prunes; Rheims has its spice cake and its spiced buns—I could go on forever.

This extraordinary list proves that French cuisine is not only a science but an art, and that this art is first and foremost our national art *par excellence*. Its reputation was already universal during the Middle Ages. And in his Commentaries, even Julius Caesar recognized that the Gauls possessed the secret for the preparation of excellent meals.

A gourmet magazine would be of great usefulness. It could report everything that the genius of fine cooking might invent every day. It could follow the progress of culinary artists and their constant efforts to deserve public acclaim. It could report the fluctuating prices of various foods products, both national and international. Such a magazine could become an easy way to correspond with other gourmets in different countries. It could establish a direct contact between Paris and the provinces for everything concerning the pleasures of the table.

* * *

The art of cooking is perhaps one of the most useful forms of diplomacy. I have been called all over the world to organize restaurant services in the most sumptuous palaces, and have always taken great care to employ French equipment, French products, and above all, French personnel, for the expansion of French cuisine worldwide is chiefly due to the thousands of French chefs who work in the four corners of the globe. They left their homes and became expatriates so that French products and the art of utilizing them could be known in the most distant countries.

It is a great satisfaction to me to have been able to contribute to this movement. During my career, I was able to implant over 2,000 French chefs all over the world. Most of them took root in their new countries, and I can say that each can be likened to grains of wheat sowed in barren ground. France is today reaping the resulting crop.

Notes Written by Escoffier Concerning His Third and Fourth Trips to America

1 9 2 6   a n d   1 9 3 0

My Third Trip to America

October 1926

ON OCTOBER 2, 1926, at the express invitation of the directors of the London Cunard Lines, I boarded the liner *Berengaria* from Cherbourg to New York, accompanied by my friend Bertrand, inspector of the restaurants of the Cunard Lines.

The weather was perfect and the sea was flat. We had no hint of sea-sickness and were therefore able to do justice to the excellent meals prepared for the passengers of this floating palace.

The *Berengaria* was the same ship, formerly called the *Imperator*, that had belonged to the Hamburg-Amerika Lines. At the end of the war it had been granted to the Cunard Lines to replace the *Lusitania*, sunk by German submarines.

I found this experience even more interesting in view of the fact that I had already been on this ship in July 1913 to organize the festivities that had been planned for the visit of His Majesty Wilhelm II, accompanied by his 125 guests. The directors of the Hamburg-Amerika Lines had asked me to come from London to direct the restaurant aboard the liner for the occasion. I have kept lasting impressions of this trip and the conversations I had with the Kaiser, despite my somber forebodings that were to come true for France the next year, in 1914. At that time the Kaiser's star was shining in full glory, and he could not believe in a change of fortune. But all things change in life! Like the colors on the face of a young woman, everything pales in life, and by 1918 there was nothing left of His Majesty's dreams of worldly luminosity but a memory.

I arrived, therefore, in New York in 1926, and was very agreeably surprised to be met at the dock by Mr. and Mrs. Scotto and many friends who had come expressly to greet me upon my arrival. After thanking them all and fulfilling my customs obligations, I was driven to the Hotel Ambassador, where I was very pleased to be reunited with Mr. Kroell, the hotel's director and an old friend from the Carlton in London, and all of his personnel, many of whom had worked for me at the Savoy, at the Carlton, and even some as far back as the Grand Hôtel in Monte Carlo.

I rested for a while and changed my clothes, and then had the pleasure of a family meal with Mr. and Mrs. Kroell, their grandchildren, and Mr. and Mrs. Scotto.

The very next day, my first outing in the morning was a visit in New York with Mr. Mongendre, the Consul of France. In most of my following visits I was accompanied by my friend Mr. Bertrand. There was so much to see and do that the fifteen days I spent there seemed very short to me! For the rest, I will simply present the following article sent to me from the United States, dating from October 16, 1926.

In Honor of Escoffier: A Brilliant Reception at the
Ritz-Carlton

October 15, 1926

All of the culinary associations of America united yesterday to honor the master they venerate and admire, Auguste Escoffier, with a magnificent reception at the Ritz-Carlton.

A great number of tables had been decorated and set up in the Grand Ballroom, and the room was thronged with people who had come to see him and express their thanks and their respect. Mr. Escoffier, smiling and friendly, had kind words for them all.

At the table of honor in the back of the room, sitting next to him, were Mr. Champion, president of the *Société Culinaire Philantropique*, Mr. Scotto, President of the Vatel Club, Mr. Gensch, Mr. La Manna, etc.

In very precise terms, Mr. Charles Scotto, who presided over this dinner, welcomed Mr. Escoffier in the name of all of the culinary associations, and, to great applause, rendered homage to the famous chef whose life, as he put it so well, was a true example for any man who had the heart to honor his profession and his art.

At the end of his speech, Mr. Scotto presented Mr. Escoffier with a beautiful golden plaque on which was inscribed two laurel branches linked by the medal of the French Légion d'Honneur, and the legend, "In honor of the Grand Maître Auguste Escoffier, from the chefs in the United States of America and all of his admirers. New York, October 15, 1926." Mr. Scotto then presented Mr. Escoffier with a book containing the signatures of all his assistants.

Mr. Escoffier, obviously very touched, then made a speech in a cheerful and paternal tone, a speech that could have been a complete conference on the art of cooking had he desired to make it longer. Mr. Escoffier spoke in such an agreeable and witty way that everyone applauded him warmly. Other speeches were made, and well appreciated, by Mr. La Manna as well as Mr. Champion, Mr. Gentsch, Mr. Scharach, and Mr. Stutsel. Mr. Scotto ended the speeches by thanking two of his "philanthropic friends," Mr. Bollaert and Mr. Weber, after which followed a splendid and unforgettable meal for the 200 guests present.

Menu

Caviar Frais d'Astrakan

Pain Grillé

Le Rossolnick

• • •

La Mousse de Sole Escortée du Cardinal des Mers à l'Américaine

• • •

Les Noisettes de Pré-Salé Favorite

Les Petits Pois à la Française

• • •

Les Perdreaux à la Casserole

• • •

La Salade Coeurs d'Endives Châtelaine

Les Belles Angevines aux Fruits d'Or

• • •

Les Mignardises

Café Moka

My Fourth Trip to America

October 1930

I RETURNED TO THE UNITED STATES on the occasion of the inauguration of the Hotel Pierre in New York. Mr. Pierre, the owner of this new palace, asked me to be the guest of honor at the banquet that was to celebrate this event.

Charles Scotto, a former student of mine and a long time friend who was now the restaurant director of the new hotel, was delighted at this initiative, and I therefore accepted their proposal.

I was in fact truly enchanted with the possibility of seeing many of my old friends and colleagues again, and perhaps once again trying to promote some of our French products, including our excellent wines, in the hope of seeing the years of Prohibition disappear and become only a bad memory.

The opening of this luxurious new hotel was planned for October 16. I therefore left Le Havre for New York on September 30 aboard the liner *Paris*, accompanied by Mr. Gérard, inspector of the restaurants for the Transatlantique Company. The crossing was excellent, and we were able to appreciate the finest meals, which were accompanied by excellent French wines until our arrival in the Prohibition Zone.

We arrived on October 7, and having thanked the captain of the ship and his officers, the restaurant chef, Léard Yves, and all of the personnel, I left the ship and was happy to be greeted by Mr. and Mrs. Scotto and several other colleagues who had come to meet me at dockside.

They drove me to the Hotel Pierre, where Mr. Pierre himself bid me welcome, thanked me for having made the trip, and asked me to make myself at home. I found myself installed in a luxurious room of this beautiful hotel, waited on with the best service that anyone could dream of.

To try to explain the days that followed, let me note the program set up by Mr. Scotto.

Program

Inaugural Dinner, Hotel Pierre, October 14, 1930
Official Opening of the Hotel, October 16, 1930
• • •
Private dinner with Mr. and Mrs. Scotto at their residence, Villa Antoinette, October 26, 1930
• • •
Champagne cocktail at the home of Mr. and Mrs. Heye to celebrate Escoffier's eighty-fifth birthday, afternoon of October 28, 1930
• • •
Dinner in celebration of Escoffier's eighty-fifth birthday, evening of October 28, 1930, in the Grand Salon of the Hotel Pierre
• • •
Dinner offered by Mr. Oscar at the Sherry Netherland, October 30, 1930
• • •
Dinner for the opening of the Club-Pierrot, October 31, 1930
• • •
Dinner offered by the German Culinary Society at the Hotel Astor, November 5, 1930
• • •
Private dinner at the home of Mr. and Mrs. Champion, November 9, 1930

• • •

*Dinner organized by the French Veterans of World War I at the Hotel
Pennsylvania, November 11, 1930*

• • •

*Dinner offered in honor of Escoffier by the Culinary Societies of New York
and of the United States, November 12, 1930*

• • •

Dinner of Hotel Managers, Hotel Commodore, November 13, 1930

• • •

*Responsibilities as Chairman of the Jury of the Sixty-second Culinary Exhibit,
New York, November 10–16, 1930*

Mushroom Cultivation in New York

During my stay in New York, I was invited by the Syndicate of Mushroom
Cultivators for an extraordinary trip to visit one of their mushroom farms,
located about four hours away from New York by train. I was very interested to see the importance that this new industry could have.

About two hundred people were invited, including hotel directors,
restaurant managers, and the largest distributors of food products from
New York, Philadelphia, and neighboring cities.

A private train was chartered and, as the trip was rather long, an excellent meal was served at noon, enabling everyone to remain in good spirits
despite the hours passed traveling.

At two o'clock the train stopped at its destination. To get all the passengers to the mushroom farm several miles away from the station, 150 cars
were lined up and waiting. When we got to the farm, we were all asked to
gather together and pose for a historic photograph.

We toured the farm until six o'clock at night admiring its size, effi-
ciency, and the quality of the products. Then six hundred guests were invited for a meal at one of the best local restaurants; dinner consisted of veal
saddle accompanied by…large platters of creamed mushrooms!

We were then taken several miles away from the restaurant to the
beautiful property of Mr. and Mrs. Dupont de Nemours, millionaires of
French origin. The gardens of their home are illuminated at night and on
this special occasion the fountains in the garden were also activated, creat-

[Photo Courtesy Evening Bulletin]

Oscar, of the Waldorf, Charles Multerer, President of the Elite Headwaiters Association and Auguste Escoffier, dean of French Hotel Chefs examining M G A Cultivated Mushrooms at Kennett Square, Pa., on Mushroom Day, October 21, 1930. On this occasion 350 hotel managers, stewards, chefs and headwaiters from New York, Newark, Atlantic City, Philadelphia, Pittsburgh and Washington visited Kennett Square, Pennsylvania, the center of America's mushroom industry.

ing an unforgettable light-and-water show worthy of the magic of any Perrault fairy tale. It was a wonderful surprise and the end of an unforgettable day. At ten o'clock I thanked the Dupont family and headed back for New York, where we arrived at 2 A.M.

Let me note that, in view of the rapid development of the mushroom industry in America, I fear that our French products may have difficulty competing with them, especially in view of the high cost of import taxes.

Return to France

My trip to New York reaching an end, I had to resign myself to leaving the country and my friends.

On November 14, 1930, I took my leave of Mr. Pierre, thanking him for his warm welcome and the proof of his friendship throughout my entire stay at his beautiful palace. I told him that I would not say good-bye, but only *au revoir*, as I dearly hoped to be able to return soon. During my stay at the Hotel Pierre, I was treated with the utmost professional esteem, and I would even say affectionate care, by the entire staff and personnel.

I then went to greet Mr. Scotto and his staff in the hotel's restaurant, and we were able to open a few bottles of champagne that had been set aside before the Prohibition to toast America and France and to express our mutual desire for world peace. I thanked them all warmly for the unforgettable time I had spent in their wonderful city.

Mr. Scotto and his wife accompanied me to the dock, where other friends awaited to wish me a safe journey back to France. I thanked them all and shook their hands, and boarded the S.S. *France* for Le Havre. The captain of the liner, Mr. Burosse, welcomed me and during the entire passage across the Atlantic, both he and his staff neglected nothing to make my trip most comfortable. I noted that the kitchen, headed by the famous chef Mr. Le Renugo, was excellent, as was as all the service provided.

Six days later I was in Le Havre and taking another train: direction— Paris!

A p p e n d i x   B

Two Letters
to Escoffier

Hotel Knickerbocker
BROADWAY AT FORTY-SECOND STREET

New York   190

JAMES B. REGAN COMPANY

le 16 Avril 1907

Cher monsieur Escoffier

Je profite de cette personne qui va entrer
au Carlton pour vous remettre en quelques lignes
. les affaires demeurent beaucoup. la situation
va-t-elle changer de phase, c'est ce que je suis
anxieux de savoir. Regan en rentrant de France
fera une vilaine figure en voyant les frais
généraux de toute la maison, que personne n'a pu
encore mettre sur un pied respectable - la Cuisine
seule, marche. Mr. Huggins nous a favorisé
deux fois, de sa visite et m'a fait ses compliments
pour la nourriture. mais tout de même, ce
n'est pas ça - si je vous disais qu'il est passé
en cuisine 150 commis entremetiers - 60 commis boulangers
40 commis g... manger. 40 .- rotisseurs, vous

penserez que j'exagère, mais c'est pourtant la pure vérité. personne ne veut travailler en Amérique sauf qu'avec des machines - Voyez que ce n'est pas gai, j'ai le plus possible moi-même car j'ai limité mon séjour - mais s'il fallait continuer, j'y renoncerais desuite -

En attendant que ma lettre vous trouve en parfaite santé, veuillez accepter mes meilleurs sentiments d'amitié et de respect.

Bien à vous

Gosten

April 16, 1907

Dear Mr. Escoffier,

I am taking advantage of the fact that this person is going to the Carlton to send you these few lines with him. Business is slowing down considerably. I am anxious to know whether this situation will change. When Regan gets back to France he will certainly be unhappy to see the company accounts that have still not been balanced in a satisfactory way. Only the kitchens are making ends meet. Mr. Higgins honored us twice with a visit and complimented me on our cooking, but I still feel it is not up to standard. If I told you that we have already seen pass through the kitchen 150 second-course cooks, 60 bakery-cooks, 40 pantry-cooks, 40 roasting-cooks, you would think that I'm exaggerating but this is the absolute truth. Nobody wants to work in America except with machines. You see that the situation is not a happy one. I am trying to do as much as I can myself, as I have shortened my stay here, but if I had to continue indefinitely, I would give up immediately.

I hope that my letter finds you in perfect health, and send you my best and most respectful regards.

Sincerely,
Gastaud

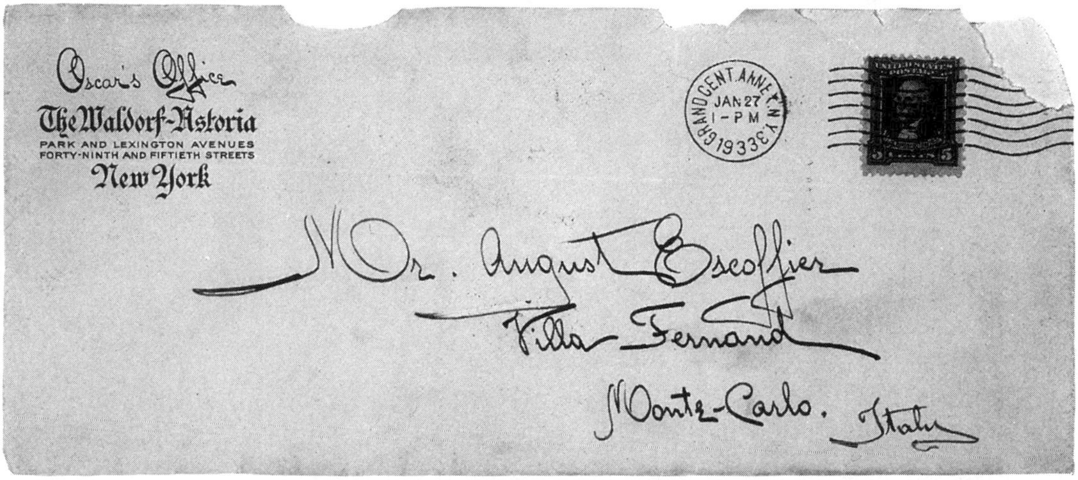
Oscar's Office
The Waldorf-Astoria
PARK AND LEXINGTON AVENUES
FORTY-NINTH AND FIFTIETH STREETS
New York
GRAND CENT. ANNEX N.Y.
JAN 27
1-PM
1933
Mr. August Escoffier
Villa Fernand
Monte-Carlo. Italy

The Waldorf-Astoria
New York

Oscar's Office

Jan 27 / 1933

Mon Cher ami Escoffier

J'ai reçu votre lettre qui ma donner beaucoup de plaisir de la recevoire, car je pense a vous bien souvent, car aprobeau de votre age l'on peud jamais savoir ce qui peud arriver d'un jour a l'autre, et concela votre lettre m'as fais beaucoup de plaisir de savoir que vous êtes toujours viffe et en bonne santée.

Cher Ami sa me fais beaucoup de peine de savoir que votre femma ats si moloreuse d'être denu dans son lit, mais j'esspère quelle ne souffre pas.

Vos affaire ici dans notre hotel vons asser bonne surtous les Banquet nous travaillons dans les jours ets nuit avec des dinner eu des Ball de Consert ets dinner privés, mais il ne faix pas comme les anneés passer c'est tous plus marcher mais enfin je tiend mes prix plus hand que vingot quel Hotel ici en Amérique.

Je suis bien content de journais vons donner de bonne nouvell de Monsieur Lugot notre Chef ich ets très bon ats un très grand travaleur ils fais une bonne Cuisina ats son travail pour les parties privés ets très bien, vous avons eu beaucoup.

206

de chance que Monsieur Gastaud avais un homme sous sa
main comme Monsieur Luget, sa nous as sauver de beaucoup
de trouble car ici en Amerique les Chef sont très rare, car
daprès mon idée je ne sais pas ou les trouver,
Cher Ami quand vous êtes a Paris donnen mes salutation a tousen
qui me conaisse et faite bien attention de ne pas atrabes froid
car vous laisser un pays qui est chaud pour aller dans
un pays froid.
    Alors cher Amé je fini ma letter en vous saluen
et en esperant que ma lettre vous trouveras en bonne
santé avec 1000 salutation de tous mon coeur Je suis
toujours votre Ami
                                Oscar

January 29, 1933

My dear friend Escoffier,

I was very pleased to receive your letter because I think of you quite often. In view of your age, one can never know what might happen from one day to the next, so I was very happy to learn from your letter that you are still active and in good health.

Dear friend, I was very distressed to learn that your wife is so unwell that she is bedridden, but I hope that she is not suffering.

Our business here at our hotel is going well enough, especially the banquets. We work every day and night on dinners at balls and private dinners, but they don't pay like in past years. It could be better, but already I have the highest prices of any other hotel in America.

I am very happy to be able to give you good news about Monsieur Lugot, our chef. He is very capable and a very hard worker. He is a good chef and his work for private parties is very good; we were very lucky that Monsieur Gastaud had a man like Monsieur Lugot at his fingertips. It saved us much trouble because here in America chefs are very rare; I don't know where to find them.

Dear friend, when you are in Paris give my regards to all who know me and be very careful not to catch cold because you are leaving a country that is warm to go to one that is cold.

Well then, dear friend, I end my letter by sending you my regards and hoping that my letter will find you in good health, with 1000 salutations from all my heart I remain always your friend.

Oscar

A p p e n d i x   C

Escoffier's Handwritten Menus

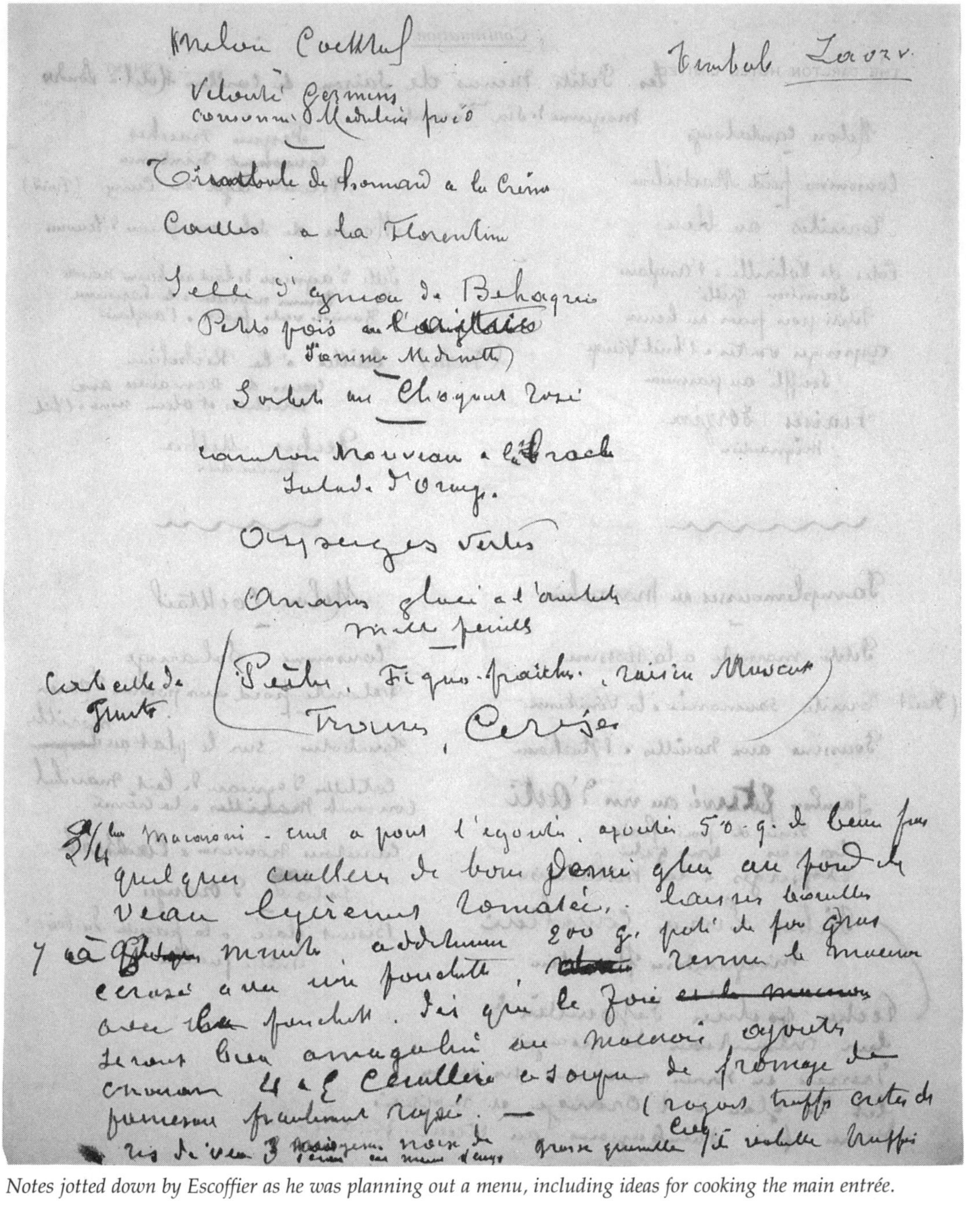

Melon Cocktail   Timbale ____

Velouté Germiny
Consommé Madrilène froid

Timbale de homard à la Crème

Coulis à la Florentine

Selle d'agneau de Béhague
Petits pois à l'anglaise

Sorbet au Champagne rosé

____ Nouveau à l'____
Salade d'Orange

Asperges vertes

____ glacé à l'____
____

Corbeille de fruits (Pêches, Figues fraîches, Raisin Muscat, ____, Cerises)

[handwritten recipe notes, largely illegible]

Notes jotted down by Escoffier as he was planning out a menu, including ideas for cooking the main entrée.

210

THE CARLTON HOTEL LIMITED   SHEET

Les Petits Menus de Saison du Carlton Hotel à Londres
Moyenne de Six Couverts

Melon Cantaloup

Consommé froid Madrilène

Truites au bleu

Côtes de Volaille à l'Anglaise
    Jambon Grillé
Petits pois frais au beurre

Asperges vertes à l'Huile Vierge
    Soufflé au parmesan

Fraises Dorzina
    Mignardise

~~~~

Figues Fraiches
Consommé Printanier
Velouté léger au Curry   (Froid)

Mousse de Sole aux queues d'Écrevisses

Selle d'agneau de lait au beurre noisette
    Pommes nouvelles à la Parisienne
    Haricots verts frais à l'Anglaise

(Froid)   Cailles à la Richelieu
    Cœurs de Romaines aux
        anchois et olives noires à l'huile

Pêches Melba
    Friandises

~~~~

Pamplemousses au Maraschino

Petite marmite à la Rossini

(Froid) Truite saumonée à la Vénitienne

Poussins aux nouilles à l'Italienne

Jambon étuvé au vin d'Asti
    Purée de pois frais
    Carottes congelées
    Asperges à la Milanaise

Pêches Lina Cavalieri
    Mignardise Florentin

Pêches pochées dépouillées de
leur manteau de pourpre
Dressées au dernier moment sur un
lit de glace à l'Orange et nappées
d'un fin sambayon au Vieux Marsala

~~~~

Melon Cocktail

Consommé Solange

Velouté froid aux pommes d'amour

Turbotin sur le plat au champagne
    morilles

Côtelettes d'agneau de lait maréchal
    concombre Morilles à la crème

Caneton nouveau à la Coucharski
    salade d'Orange

Biscuit glacé à la fraisette du bois
    mille feuilles

Seasonal menus for six served at the Carlton Hotel.

Menu, Dîner servi à Sa Majesté le Roi Léopold II
de Belgique

Sa Majesté venu à Londres, voyageant incognito était descendu au Carlton Hôtel, pour un très court séjour, on était en Juin.

Voici le Menu du Dîner qui lui fut servi le soir de son arrivée :

6 couverts

Caviar frais
Galettes feuilletées

Melon fine Champagne servi en coupes

Consommé Royal

Graves Mouzzole   Turbotin Bonne Femme
Dry
                         Cailles Orientale

Clos de Vougeot   Selle d'agneau de Galles poêlée
C   1889
                              Petits pois au laitues
                              Pommes Bergerette

                         Mousse de tomate au blanc de Poulet en gelée

Champagne   Salade d'asperges vertes

Pommery et Greno   Soufflé au fromage Périgourdine
cuvée réservée
1892   Pêches Melba

                         Gaufrettes Flamandes

                              Café Mokka

Liqueurs { Grande Fine Champagne (Souvenir de Napoléon)
         { vieille Chartreuse du couvent.

A. S.

Dinner served to his Majesty Leopold II of Belgium on the evening of his arrival at the Carlton Hotel, while he was making a brief, incognito trip to London.

Diners servis à S.M. Alphonse XIII   66   1912
au Carlton Hôtel de Londres.

Melon   Melon Caviar frais

Petite marmite à la moelle   Rossolnick
Soles Bosca

Selle d'agneau de Galles   Turbotin au coulis d'écrevisse
Laitues farcies Valencienne
                               Filet de bœuf poêlé
Poularde à la Broche   tomates au gratin, haricots verts
Cœurs de Romaine   pommes midinettes

Aubergines à l'Orientale   Dindonneau farci à l'anglaise
                                  Salade de Laitues
Biscuit glacé à la vanille
pêches — framboises   fonds d'artichauts à la périgourdine
    friandises
                                  Soufflé au Curaçao
Corbeille de fruits   friandises

                               Pêches — fruits figues raisins

Dinners served to his Majesty Alphonse XIII of Spain at the Carlton Hotel, 1912.

213

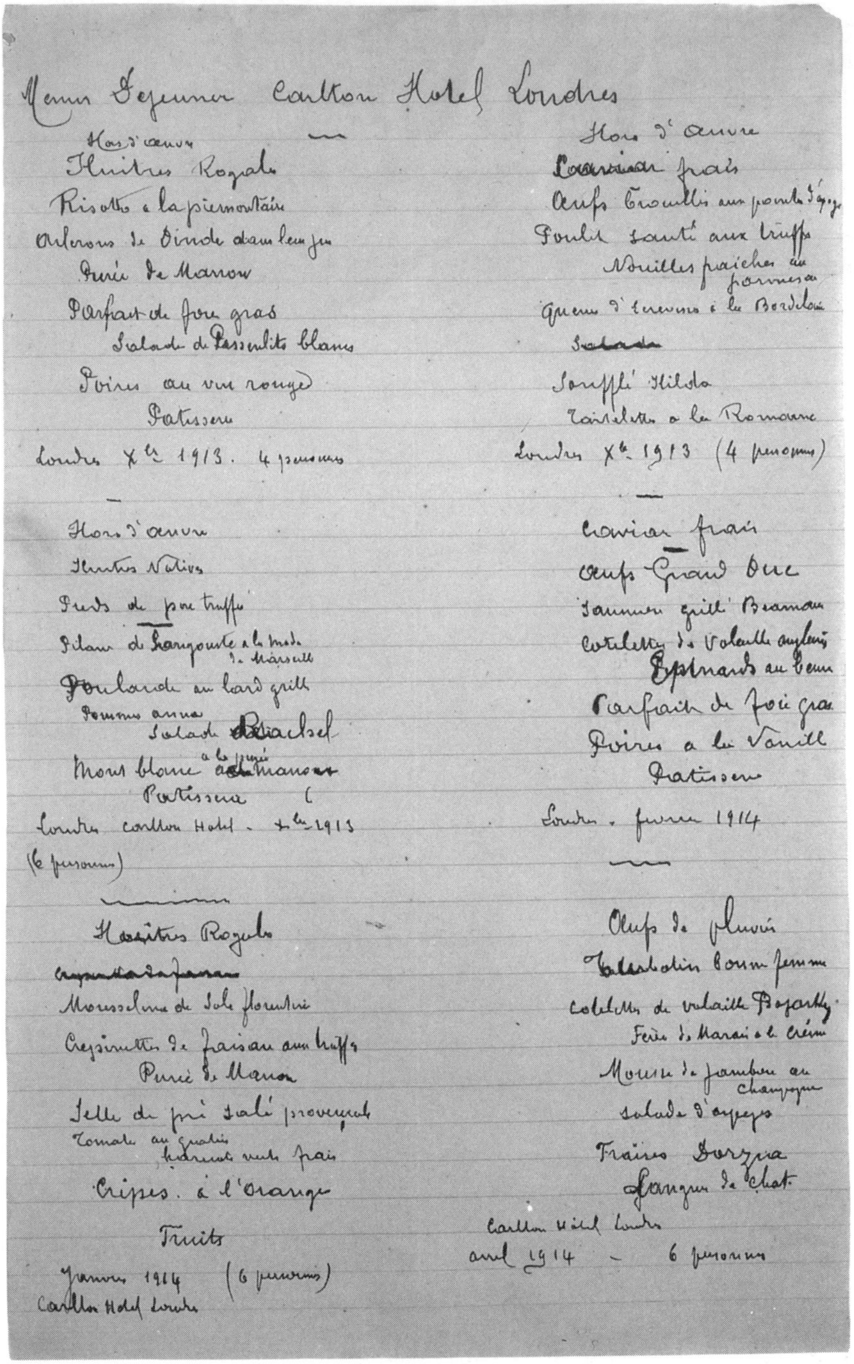

Menu Déjeuner Carlton Hotel Londres

Hors d'oeuvre
Huîtres Royales
Risotto à la piémontaise
Ailerons de Dinde dans leur jus
Purée de Marron
Parfait de foie gras
Salade de Pissenlits blancs
Poires au vin rouge
Patisserie
Londres Xbre 1913. 4 personnes

Hors d'oeuvre
Caviar frais
Oeufs brouillés aux pointes d'asperges
Poulet sauté aux truffes
Nouilles fraîches au parmesan
Queue d'écrevisses à la Bordelaise
Salade
Soufflé Hilda
Tartelettes à la Romaine
Londres Xbre 1913 (4 personnes)

Hors d'oeuvre
Huîtres Natives
Pieds de porc truffés
Filets de Langouste à la mode de Marseille
Poularde au lard grillé
Pommes Anna
Salade Rachel
Mont blanc à la purée de marron
Patisserie
Londres Carlton Hotel - Xbre 1913
(6 personnes)

Caviar frais
Oeufs Grand Duc
Saumon grillé Béarnaise
Cotelettes de volaille anglaise
Epinards au beurre
Parfait de foie gras
Poires à la Vanille
Patisserie
Londres. février 1914

Huîtres Royales
Mousseline de Sole florentine
Crepinettes de faisan aux truffes
Purée de Marron
Selle de pré salé provençale
Tomates au gratin
haricots verts frais
Crêpes à l'orange
Fruits
Janvier 1914 (6 personnes)
Carlton Hotel Londres

Oeufs de pluvier
Galantine bonne femme
Cotelettes de volaille Pojarsky
Fèves de Marais à la crème
Mousse de jambon au champagne
Salade d'asperges
Fraises Gorzia
Langues de chat
Carlton Hotel Londres
avril 1914 - 6 personnes

Lunch menus served at the Carlton Hotel, London 1914.

Caviar frais
Poule au pot
Timbalin grillé aux lardons
   Sauce Béarnaise
Filets de Perdreaux à la Rossini
   Nouilles à l'Italienne
Asperges de serre
Poires à la vanille
   Crème Chantilly
Londres X^bre nov 1913 - 6 personnes

———

Hors d'œuvre Russe
Petite Marmite
Bisque d'écrevisses
Truite au bleu
Selle d'agneau de Galles Soubise
haricots verts de serre au beurre
Pommes Nana
Poulardes Truffées
   Salade de laitue
Asperges de Caume
Cœur sensible aux fraises
   Mignardises
Londres Mars 1914 - 10 personnes

———

Consommé Talleyrand
Timbale de queues d'écrevisses à la crème
Selle d'agneau de lait Bordelaise
   haricots verts frais au beurre
Bécassines casserole
   Salade de laitue
Pêches du Cap Melba
Londres Janvier 1914 - 3 couverts

Huîtres Royales
Bortsch
   Petits pâtés chauds
Saumon Walewska
Cailles en pilaw
Râbles de Lièvre à la crème
   Purée de châtaigne
Haricots verts frais au beurre
Soufflé Montmorency
   Paillettes vanillées
Londres X^bre 1913 — 6 Personnes

———

H. d'œuvre
   caviar frais
Consommé Vladimir
Petits Pâtés chauds
Sole Coquelin
Filets de poulet aux truffes
   Purée de Marron
Sarcelles au porto
   Salade d'Orange
~~Fraises Timbales rapées~~
Pointes d'asperges à la Crème
Biscuit glacé Caprice
   Langues de chat
Londres Février 1914 (6 personnes

———

Consommé Réjane
Homard cardinal
Côtelette d'agneau de lait anglaise
   Pointes d'asperges au beurre
Rouge de Rivière à la presse
   Salade d'orange
Soufflé Anisette
   Fruit
Londres Mars 1914   2 personnes

Courants

Menus du Restaurant du Carlton Hotel Londres

Dîner · 4 à 6 personnes   Dîner 8 à 10 personnes

Natives   Caviar Frais

Petite Marmite   Rondrink

Filets de Sole Nantua   Truite au bleu

Côtes de Volaille à l'anglaise   Selle de veau Orloff

Jambon grillé   Concombres au beurre
Pointes d'asperges au beurre

Paté de grives   Bécasses au fumet

Salade de laitue   Salade Lorette

Mandarines Givrées   Asperges Vertes

Friandises   Soufflé glacé au chocolat

Février 1914   Londres   Londres février 1914   Mille feuilles

H. d'œuvre   H. d'œuvre

Saumon fumé   Grapp fruit

Consommé Solange   Velouté Tosca

Mousseline d'Ecrélans au Cury   Rougets grillés Diable

Selle de chevreuil Cumberland   Ris de veau poêlés

Purée de Marron   Chicorée à la crème

Chapon Truffé   Canards sauvages au sang

Salade de Blanc de céleri   Salade d'Orange

Haricots verts de serre à l'anglaise   Soufflé au parmesan

Poires à la Bohémienne   Charlotte de pommes

Mignardises   Mousse chantilly

Janvier 1914 — 6 à 8 personnes   Janvier 1914 ——— 6 personnes

H. d'œuvre   H. d'œuvre

Jambon fumé   Huitres. Côte Rouge

Bisque d'écrevisses   Potage Iris

Sole à la Russe   Sole à la Normande

Côtelettes d'agneau Maréchal   Selle d'agneau de Pauillac persillé
Petits pois frais   haricots verts à l'anglaise
Pommes Byron

Pâté de foie gras   Faisan Souvaroff
Salade de laitue   Salade Endive

Coupe Mireille   Crêpes Suzette
Friandises

Londres février 1914.   Londres 6 janvier 1914

Menus for four to six and eight to ten served at the Carlton Hotel, London 1914.

216

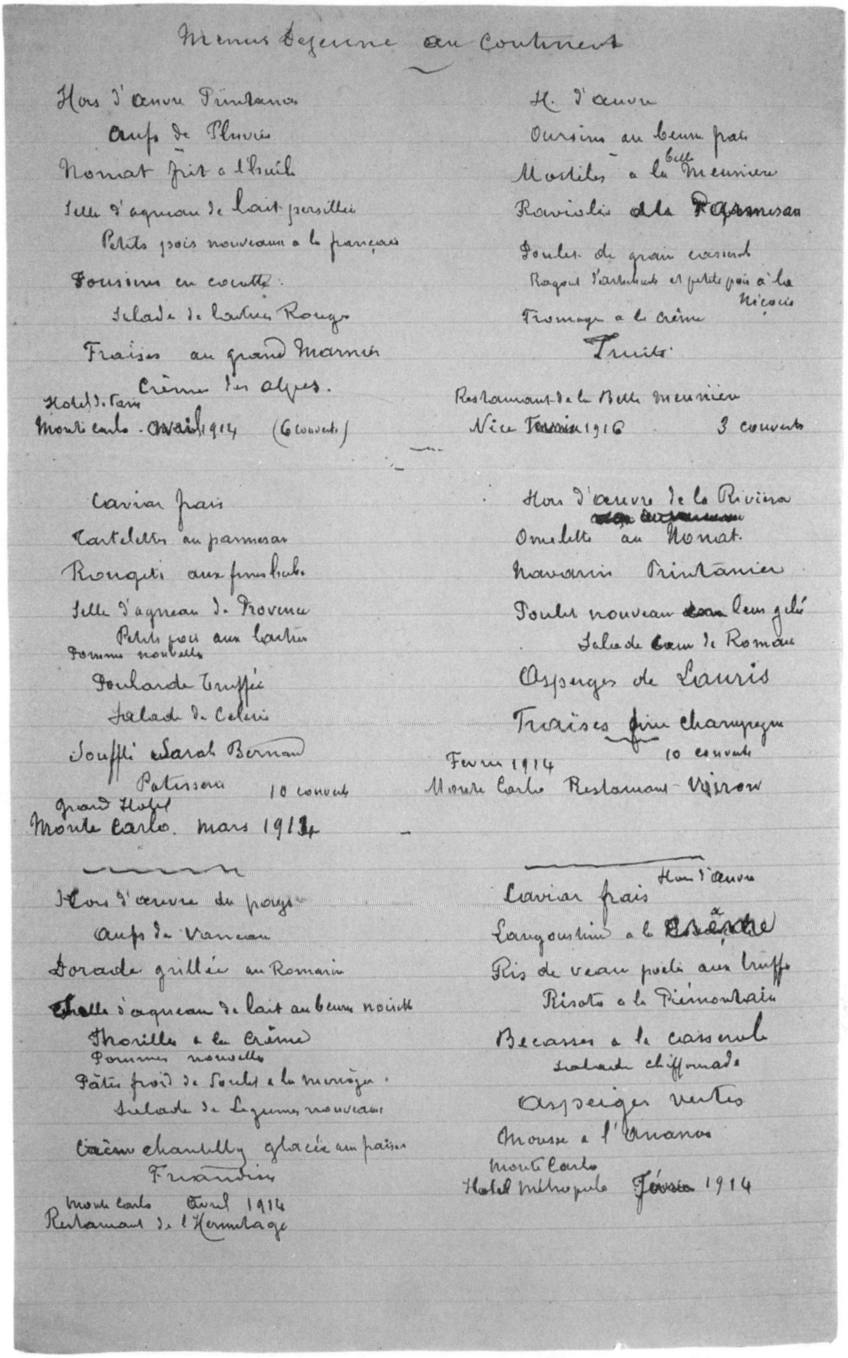

Menus Dejeune au Continent

Hors d'oeuvre Printanier
Oeufs de Pluvier
Nonat frit a l'huile
Selle d'agneau de lait persillée
Petits pois nouveaux a la française
Poussins en cocotte
Salade de laitues Rouges
Fraises au grand Marnier
Crême des alpes.
Hotel de Paris
Monte Carlo avril 1914 (6 couverts)

H. d'oeuvre
Oursins au beurre frais
Moules a la belle Meunière
Raviolis de Parmesan
Poulet de grain cassarole
Ragout d'artichauts et petits pois à la Niçoise
Fromage a la crême
Fruits
Restaurant de la Belle Meunière
Nice Fevrier 1916 3 couverts

Caviar frais
Cartelettes au parmesan
Rougets aux fines herbes
Selle d'agneau de Provence
Petits pois aux laitues
Pommes nouvelles
Poularde truffée
Salade de Celeri
Soufflé Sarah Bernhardt
Patisseries 10 couverts
Grand Hotel
Monte Carlo. mars 1914

Hors d'oeuvre de la Riviera
Omelette au Nonat
Navarin Printanier
Poulet nouveau en beurre gelé
Salade de coeurs de Romaine
Asperges de Lauris
Fraises fine champagne
Fevrier 1914 10 couverts
Monte Carlo Restaurant Ciro's

Hors d'oeuvre du pays
Oeufs de Vanneau
Dorade grillée au Romarin
Selle d'agneau de lait au beurre noisette
Morilles a la crême
Pommes nouvelles
Pâté froid de Poulet a la Menagère
Salade de Legumes nouveaux
Crême chantilly glacée aux fraises
Friandises
Monte Carlo Avril 1914
Restaurant de l'Hermitage

Caviar frais Hors d'oeuvre
Langoustines a la [illegible]
Ris de veau poele aux truffes
Risotto a la Piemontaise
Becasses a la cassarole
Salade chiffonade
Asperges vertes
Mousse a l'Ananas
Monte Carlo
Hotel Metropole Fevrier 1914

Continental lunch menus.

Spring Menu
with
Wines from The Savoy Cellars
£64.00

The creative talent and expertise of Werner Wissmann (River Restaurant Sommelier) and Anton Edelmann (Maître Chef des Cuisines) have combined to produce this seasonal menu with wines from The Savoy Cellars.

They believe that enormous pleasure may be derived from a perfect marriage of wine and food. Each of the dishes and wines were tasted until a match which enhanced each of the courses was found.

One glass of the wines chosen will be served with the selected courses. Should you not care for one or all of these wines, the selection may be varied or the menu taken with a wine of your choice.

Compressé de Homard et Saumon Cru
(Lobster and Salmon terrine)
Mâcon Lugny, Les Genièvres (Louis Latour) 1994

Bouillon d'Asperges et son Ravioli
(Asparagus Broth with its Ravioli)

Risotto aux Truffes d'Eté
(Summer Truffle Risotto)
Muscat (Schlumberger) 1993

Jumelle d'Agneau "Nouvelle Saison" Savoyarde
(Fillet of New Season's Lamb, Lamb's Kidneys and Sweetbreads on a Potato Savoyarde with a Basil Sauce)
Château Roudier (Montagne-St. Emilion) 1989

Compote de Rhubarb et son Petit Soufflé
(Rhubarb Compote with Rhubarb Soufflé)
Muscat de Beaumes de Venise

Frivolités et Café Filtre Savoy

Friday 24th May 1996

Price is inclusive of the selected wines, Value Added Tax and Service.
The menu price exclusive of wines is at £58.50

A current menu from the Savoy Hotel, London, exemplifying Escoffier's continuing influence.

Appendix D

People in Escoffier's Life

Albert Edward, Prince of Wales

1841–1910

Edward VII, King of Great Britain and Ireland, from 1901 to 1910

THE ELDEST SON of Queen Victoria and Prince Albert, Edward was created Prince of Wales almost immediately after his birth. As a youth he traveled widely on the Continent and visited the United States and Canada and the Middle East. In 1863 he married Alexandra, daughter of Christian IX of Denmark. They had six children. A liberal patron of the arts and sciences, he became a leader of fashionable society and an enthusiastic sportsman. He was very dedicated to the cuisine of Escoffier, and was often seen at all the best restaurants. He was known for his love of life, women, and extravagant living. He succeeded to the throne at the age of fifty-nine and was crowned on August 9, 1902. As King of Great Britain and Ireland he took a deep interest in foreign policy and by his travels helped to promote international understanding. The popularity he attained in France smoothed the way for the Anglo-French entente of 1904. He died in 1910 and was succeeded by his eldest surviving son, George V.

Sarah Bernhardt

1844–1923

SARAH BERNHARDT was the stage name of Rosine Bernard, a famous actress during the Third Republic. She was brought up in a convent until the age of thirteen, after which she entered the Paris Conservatory. She made her debut at the Comédie Française at the age of eighteen, but only began to attract attention for her performance in Coppee's *Le Passant* at the Odéon in 1869. With the Comédie Française (1872-1880) she attained her full stature with superb portrayals of Phèdre (1876) and of Dona Sol in Hugo's *Hernani* (1877). Renowned for her golden voice, she was considered the queen of French romantic and classical tragedy. Oscar Wilde called her "the divine Sarah," a designation by which she became universally known. In 1880 she began her tours of England, Europe, and the United States. She managed several theatres in Paris before leasing the Théâtre des Nations, renaming it the Théâtre Sarah Bernhardt. In 1912 she appeared in the silent films *La Dame aux Camélias* and *Queen Elizabeth*. Her leg was amputated in 1915, but her career continued and she made numerous "farewell" tours. An accomplished painter, poet, and sculptor, she also wrote plays in which she appeared.

Dame Nellie Melba

1859–1931

BORN HELEN PORTER MITCHELL, Melba was a famous soprano of Australian origin. After studying in Paris, she made her operatic debut in Brussels in 1887. Famous for her lyric and coloratura roles, she sang regularly at Covent Garden in London from 1888 to 1926 and intermittently with the Metropolitan Opera Company in New York City from 1893 to 1910, as well as making appearances in Australia and many other parts of the world. She was made Dame of the British Empire in 1918.

César Ritz

1850–1918

THE SON OF A SWISS PEASANT, César Ritz rose to become the manager and owner of some of the grandest and most sumptuous hotels in the world. In order to learn the restaurant business Ritz started working at first as a waiter, at the finest restaurant in Paris, the Voisin, until the siege of Paris of 1870 caused such shortages of food and fuel that the Voisin had to close. After the siege he worked as *maître d'hôtel* at the Hotel Splendide in Paris, where he again came in contact with the celebrated and wealthy. From 1877 to 1887 he managed the summer season at the luxurious Hôtel National in Lucerne, Switzerland. He was also appointed general manager of the Grand Hôtel in Monte Carlo in 1877, where he first met Escoffier. Their deep friendship and professional collaboration would last over thirty years. Between them, they established the reputation first of the London Savoy (1890–1897) and later of the Carlton Hotel in London. In 1898 Ritz opened the palatial Ritz Hotel on the Place Vendôme in Paris, and at the same time managed other great hotels in London, Rome, Italy, Germany, and Switzerland. His endless energy and innovative methods of hotel management made his hotels and his name synonymous with elegance, comfort, and great luxury.

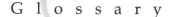

Glossary

agneau lamb (young, but weaned).

agneau de Pauillac Pauillac house lamb (unweaned).

agneau de lait house or young lamb (unweaned).

aigre-doux sweet-and-sour (sauce), bittersweet (fruit or drink).

Alexandra name given to several dishes (consommé, fillets of sole, etc.) served with a sauce and garnished with a thin slice of truffle and asparagus.

alsacienne (à l') pork, pheasant, duck, goose, or egg dishes garnished with sauerkraut, ham, salted bacon, Strasbourg sausage, etc. Also used to describe timbales (pies and terrines containing *foie gras*), and fruit tarts covered with an egg mixture.

américaine (à l') name given to a classic dish of shellfish, particularly lobster, created by Pierre Fraisse, a French chef known as Peters, who settled in Paris about 1860 after having worked in America. Also applied to fish garnishes containing thin slices of lobster tail and sauce américaine.

amande verte fresh almond.

amandes grillées toasted almonds.

ananas pineapple.

anchois anchovy.

angevin (e) from the city of Angers.

anglaise (à l') description given to vegetables, meat, and fish prepared according to British gastronomy; vegetables are often steamed, boiled, or poached in a white stock; meat or fish are coated in breadcrumbs before frying, etc.

Anna name of potato dish created by Adolphe Dugléré to accompany roast meat and poultry, dedicated to Anna Deslions, woman of fashion during the Second Empire.

Argenteuil   name given to dishes with a sauce or garnish containing asparagus.

arlésienne (à l')   description given to dishes with a garnish of fried eggplants, sautéed tomatoes and fried onion rings.

asperge   asparagus.

aubergine   eggplant.

aveline   hazelnut or filbert.

Béarnaise   a hot creamy sauce made from egg yolks and reduced vinegar, beaten together over a low heat and mixed with butter, usually served with grilled meat or fish.

béatilles   mixture of white meat and mushroom used to make pâtés or garnish bouchées.

bécasse (des bois)   woodcock.

barquerolle   small sculling boat; a small boat-shaped tart.

beau, belle   beautiful.

beurre fondu   melted butter.

biscuit glacé   a light ice cream made up of rectangular layers of frozen fruit custard, served in slices.

blé noir   buckwheat, Saracen corn.

blanc de poulet   chicken breast.

blanc de romaine   heart of Romaine lettuce.

boeuf   beef.

bombe   a light ice cream molded in round molds or conical-shaped molds with a round dome.

bordelaise (à la)   name given to a wide range of dishes (eggs, fish, shellfish, kidneys, steak, etc.) that use such ingredients as bone marrow, shallots, and wine.

bouchée   puff pastry shell.

bouquetière   flower girl.

bourgeoise (à la)   term used for dishes that are typical family meals without a set recipe, especially braised meat served with carrots, onions, and bacon.

bretonne (à la)   dish having a garnish of whole or puréed haricot (navy) beans, of which Britanny is a famous producer.

broche (à la)   spit (roasted on a spit).

bruxelloise (à la)   garnish consisting of stewed brussels sprouts, braised chicory, and potatoes, served with small joints of sautéed or roasted meat, or eggs.

caille   quail.

Calissons   petit fours made of almond paste with a glazed icing, a specialty of Aix-en-Provence.

canard   duck.

caneton de Rouen   Rouen duckling.

capucin   a small savory tartlet filled with Gruyère choux pastry and served as a hot entrée.

Cardinal des Mers   a fish dish garnished with lobster escalopes (or sometimes slices of truffle) or coated with a white sauce containing lobster stock.

Cardinalisé   Used to describe shellfish cooked in stock— their shells become red, like a cardinal's robe. Also used for other "red" dishes including iced desserts containing red fruit.

Carmélite (à la)   cold dish consisting of chicken suprêmes covered with chaud-froid sauce, garnished with slices of truffle and dressed with a mousseline of crayfish and crayfish tails.

Carmen   any of various dishes,

including consommé, eggs, or fillets of sole that contain tomato or pimento, and generally a highly seasoned garnish in the Spanish style.

cerise   cherry.

châtelaine (à la)   a method of garnishing simple dishes, with chestnuts or artichoke hearts for example, to add refinement.

champignon   mushroom.

Chantilly   fresh cream beaten to the consistency of a mousse, sweetened and flavored with vanilla or other flavors.

chaud-froid   a dish that is prepared as a hot dish but served cold. Chaud-froids are pieces of meat, poultry, fish, or game coated with brown or white sauce, then glazed with aspic.

chevreuil   venison.

Clamart   any of various dishes that include green peas, either whole or puréed.

cocotte   stewpan, casserole (also: courtesan, kept woman).

coeur d'artichaut   artichoke heart.

coeur de céleri   celery heart.

coeur de Romaine   heart of Romaine lettuce.

concombre   cucumber.

corbeille   basket.

coulis   purée.

créole (à la)   name given to numerous sweet and savory dishes inspired by West Indian cookery; in particular a method of preparing rice.

crêpes au blé noir   buckwheat pancakes.

crépinette   flat sausage.

crevettes   shrimp.

délice   sweet delicacy.

daube (en)   stewed or braised.

diablé (e)   deviled.

diable (à la)   name given to dishes of meat, poultry, fish, and shellfish, etc. that are seasoned, usually coated with mustard, dipped in egg, coated with bread crumbs, grilled, and served with a deviled sauce.

doré   golden.

dragée   sugar-coated almond.

du pays   native.

en branches   in leaves or branches.

écossaise (à l')   particularly used to describe a Scottish soup (Scotch broth); also used for various dishes containing salmon.

écrevisse   crayfish.

éperlan   smelt, a small trout-like fish.

épinards   spinach.

estragon   tarragon.

florentine (à la)   method of preparation used for fish, white meat, or eggs in which spinach (and usually mornay sauce) is used.

foie gras   fattened goose or duck liver.

fond d'artichauts   artichoke heart.

forestière (à la)   method of preparing small cuts of meat or chicken garnished with mushrooms (chanterelles, morels, or cèpes) cooked in butter, usually accompanied by potato noisettes or rissoles and blanched brown bacon pieces.

française (à la)   describing a preparation of joints of meat served with asparagus tips, braised lettuce, cauliflower florets coated with hollandaise sauce, and small potato nests filled with diced mixed vegetables.

friandise   sweet delicacy.

frivolité   a highly seasoned savory, such as a canapé, served at the beginning or end of a meal.

fromage   cheese.

fumet   a highly flavored, fairly concentrated essence of fish, poultry, meat etc.

gaufrette bretonne   wafer from Brittany.

gelée   jelly or aspic.

Grand Veneur   term used to describe dishes of ground game, roasted or sautéed, covered with venison sauce (a poivrade sauce with red currant jelly and fresh cream).

grecque (à la)   describing dishes of Greek origin but more loosely used for dishes inspired by Mediterranean cuisine.

guignard (e)   unlucky person, Jonah.

haricot rouge   red kidney bean.

haricot vert   French green bean.

homard   lobster.

hongroise (à la)   in the Hungarian style, describing dishes that contain paprika.

huître   oyster.

Impératrice (à l')   name given to various sweet or savory dishes characterized by the richness of their ingredients.

indienne (à l')   name given to many dishes of curried fish, eggs, meat, or poultry, usually served with rice.

italienne (à l')   name given to dishes that are either dressed with Italian sauce (mushroom, ham, and chopped herbs) or garnished, with artichoke hearts or macaroni. Also name given to dishes typical of Italian cookery.

jambon   ham.

japonaise (à la)   name given to various dishes containing Chinese artichokes (called Japanese artichokes in French).

laitance   soft roe.

langouste   spiny or rock lobster.

langoustine   prawn.

Lavallière   name given to several great culinary dishes, although it is not known whether they were dedicated to Louise de la Vallière, mistress of Louis XIV, or to a famous actress in the Belle Epoque.

légèrement   lightly.

madrilène (à la)   name given to a poultry consommé enriched with tomato pulp, sometimes served hot, but usually served chilled or, iced in the Spanish tradition.

marquise   any of various delicate desserts, such as chocolate marquise (half-way between a mousse and a parfait) or granita (a type of Italian sorbet) with Chantilly cream.

marron   chestnut.

Melba   the name of various dishes dedicated to Dame Nellie Melba, the famous 19th-century Australian opera singer.

merlan   whiting.

meunière (à la)   a method of cooking used for all types of fish; they are lightly floured and fried in butter, then sprinkled with lemon juice, noisette butter and parsley.

mignardise   sweet delicacy.

mignon   a dish of sweetbreads or small cuts of meat, which are sautéed, coated with Madeira-flavored demi-glace sauce, and served with artichoke hearts filled with garden peas and topped with slices of truffle.

mignonnette small circles or ovals of meat or forcemeat.

moëlle bone marrow.

Montmorency name given to various savory or sweet dishes that include the sour Montmorency cherries.

Montpensier (à la) name given to various savory or sweet dishes that may have been dedicated to the Duchesse de Montpensier (1627–1693) but were more probably dedicated to the fifth son of Louis Philippe.

moscovite (à la) term describing various preparations inspired by Russian cookery or perfected by French chefs who had worked in Russia in the 19th century.

mousse a frothy molded preparation for several people, served hot or cold.

mousse à la fraise strawberry mousse.

mousse de jambon ham mousse.

mousseline single servings of a mousse preparation, usually the size of quenelle.

mousseron edible mushroom.

mouton mutton.

napolitaine (à la) a method of serving buttered macaroni or spaghetti either in tomato sauce or with peeled, chopped, and deseeded tomatoes, sprinkled with grated cheese.

noisettes d'agneau small circles of meat cut from the lamb's neck.

normande (à la) describing various dishes based on the cooking of Normandy or made using typically Norman products, such as butter, fresh cream, seafood, apples, cider, and Calvados.

orientale (à l') name given to many dishes inspired by the cooking of Turkey and the Balkans and containing numerous ingredients and spices from the Mediterranean region (eggplants, tomatoes, rice, saffron, onions, peppers, etc.).

orléanaise (à l') describing large cuts of meat garnished with braised endives and *maître d'hôtel* potatoes.

Orléans name given to tartlets of eggs garnished with bone marrow and truffle, or with diced chicken in tomato sauce.

ortolan ortolan, small bird of the finch family.

paillettes puff-pastry sticks or straws.

panse first stomach (of a ruminant).

papillote (en) food cooked in a paper case.

parisienne (à la) preparations that are typical of the classic repertoire of Parisian restaurants (potato noisettes with herbs, for example).

Parmentier various culinary preparations based on potatoes, named after Antoine Augustin Parmentier(1737–1813), enthusiastic supporter of this vegetable for its nutritional value.

parmesan Parmesan cheese.

patate douce sweet potato.

paupiette thin slice of meat, fish, or cabbage spread thin with a layer of forcemeat and rolled up.

perdreau young partridge.

perdrix adult partridge.

pêche peach.

périgourdin (e) of the Périgord region of France

périgourdine (à la) describing egg, meat, poultry, or game dishes served with a périgourdine sauce consisting of demi-glace enriched with foie gras purée and diced or sliced truffle.

petit pois small green peas.

petite marmite stockpot.

piémontaise (à la) describing various dishes that incorporate a risotto, sometimes accompanied by white Piedmont truffles.

pigeonneau young pigeon.

pluvier plover, a shore bird.

poêlé pan-fried.

poché poached.

pointes d'asperges asparagus tips.

poire pear.

pomme apple; also used to indicate any round-shaped object.

pomme de terre potato.

pommes d'amour plum tomatoes.

pommes noisettes potatoes cut into large, nut-size balls.

Pompadour dishes dedicated to Jeanne Poisson, Marquise de Pompadour (1721–1764), French royal favorite and mistress of Louis XV. She played an important role in the King's life and was a notable influence in the world of art, including cookery.

pot-au-feu beef stew.

poulard fattened chicken.

poulet chicken.

pré salé salt meadow lamb.

printanière describing various dishes which are garnished with a mixture of spring vegetables, usually tossed in butter.

provençale (à la) describing numerous preparations inspired by the cookery of Provence, in which olive oil, tomato, and garlic predominate.

rôtisseur chef in charge of roasting meats.

Rachel stage name of the great tragic actress Elizabeth Félix (1821–1858), mistress of famous gastronome, Doctor Véron.

raifort horseradish.

raisin grapes.

Renaissance (à la) a cookery term describing a large braised or roast cut of meat or chicken garnished with small heaps of different vegetables.

Richelieu a garnish for large cuts of meat comprising stuffed tomatoes, mushrooms, braised lettuce, and fried new potatoes. Also a method of cooking sole. These and other dishes were dedicated to the Duc de Richelieu (the Cardinal's grandnephew).

rissolé (e) browned or fried.

riz rice.

rouennaise (à la) a description applied mainly to preparations of duck or duckling, for which Rouen is famous.

rouget mullet.

sablé shortbread cookie.

Saint-Germain name given to various dishes containing green peas; named after the Comte de Saint-Germain, war minister under Louis XV.

Sainte-Alliance description of several famous dishes inspired by the festivities surrounding the signing of the Treaty of Paris (1815) by the sovereigns who had conquered Napoleon I.

sarrasin buckwheat, Saracen corn.

saumon fumé   smoked salmon.

selle d'agneau   saddle of lamb.

selle d'agneau de Pauillac   saddle of Pauillac house lamb.

selle de veau   saddle of veal.

serre   greenhouse.

siège   seat, center (of learning), siege (military).

soubise (à la)   name given to dishes containing an onion sauce or purée, in honor of Charles de Rohan, Prince of Soubise and marshal of France in the 18th century.

soufflé   soufflé; a light and frothy baked egg dish.

soufflé au fromage   cheese soufflé.

sous la cendre   braised in hot ashes.

souverain(e)   sovereign.

strasbourgeoise (à la)   describing a dish consisting of large cuts of braised or fried meat garnished with sauerkraut, bacon, and slices of foie gras.

suédoise   a term describing various dishes reminiscent of Scandinavian cookery.

suc   juice.

suprêmes d'écrevisse   crayfish fillets

suprêmes de poulet   chicken breasts.

suprêmes de rouget   mullet fillets.

terrine   terrine (earthenware vessel), or the pâté made in such a terrine.

timbale   timbale (a deep bowl, sometimes a mold).

Tortoni   a famous café, restaurant and ice-cream parlour, opened in Paris from 1789 to 1893.

tortue claire   clear turtle soup.

toulousaine (à la)   a garnish for poached or pot-roasted poultry, or a filling for tarts and vols-au-vent. Also used for dishes from southwestern France.

truffe   truffle.

truite de rivière   river trout.

truite saumonée   salmon trout.

turbotin   small turbot.

veau   veal.

velouté   a creamy smooth soup.

Victoria   a number of dishes and sauces dedicated to Queen Victoria, all characterized by rich ingredients or an elegant presentation.

vol-au-vent   a round case of puff pastry, having a pastry lid, that is filled after baking with meat, fish, or poultry bound with sauce, and served very hot as an entrée or hors d'oeuvres.

volaille   poultry.

Walewska (à la)   name given to fish poached in a fumet, garnished with a slice of lobster and thinly sliced truffle, coated with Mornay sauce, finished with lobster butter and glazed in the oven. Dedicated to Count Walewska, natural son of Napoleon I and Marie Walewska, who was ambassador to London and Minister for foreign affairs under Napoleon III.

Bibliography

Donon, Joseph. *French Classic Cuisine*. New York: Alfred A. Knopf, 1961.

Escoffier, Auguste. *The Complete Guide to the Art of Modern Cookery* [Le Guide Culinaire]. H.L Cracknell and R.J. Kaufmann, translators. New York: Van Nostrand Reinhold, 1979.

Herbodeau, Eugène, and Paul Thalamas. *Georges Auguste Escoffier*. London: Practical Press Ltd, 1955.

Larousse Gastronomique. Jennifer Harvey Lang, editor. New York: Crown Publishers, 1988.

Parienté, Henriette, and Geneviéve de Ternant. *La Fabuleuse Histoire de la Cuisine Française*. Paris: Editions O.D.I.L, 1981.

Ritz, Marie. *César Ritz*. Torrento: Editions Tallandier, J.B. Libbcott Co., 1948.

Shaw, Timothy. *The World of Escoffier*. New York: The Vendome Press, 1995.

Trager, James. *The Food Chronology*. New York: Henry Holt Company, 1995.

Chronology

*The Life and Times of
Auguste Escoffier*

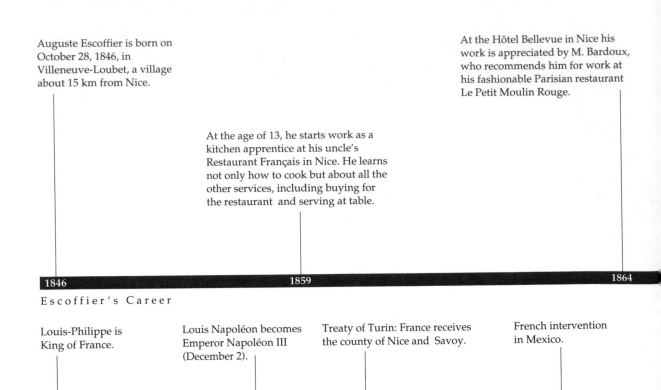

Auguste Escoffier is born on October 28, 1846, in Villeneuve-Loubet, a village about 15 km from Nice.

At the Hôtel Bellevue in Nice his work is appreciated by M. Bardoux, who recommends him for work at his fashionable Parisian restaurant Le Petit Moulin Rouge.

At the age of 13, he starts work as a kitchen apprentice at his uncle's Restaurant Français in Nice. He learns not only how to cook but about all the other services, including buying for the restaurant and serving at table.

| 1846 | 1859 | 1864 |

Escoffier's Career

Louis-Philippe is King of France.

Louis Napoléon becomes Emperor Napoléon III (December 2).

Treaty of Turin: France receives the county of Nice and Savoy.

French intervention in Mexico.

Revolution in Paris—abdication of Louis-Philippe (February 24). Proclamation of the Second Republic. Louis-Napoléon Bonaparte elected President (December 10).

War in Italy against Austria, leading to the Italian unification in 1861.

| 1846 | 1848 | 1852 | 1859 | 1860 | 1863 |

World Events

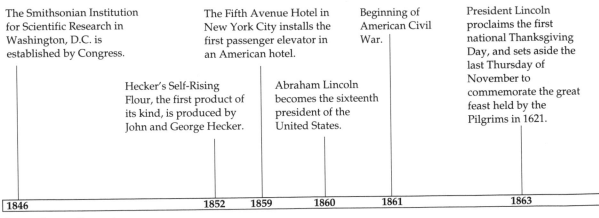

The Smithsonian Institution for Scientific Research in Washington, D.C. is established by Congress.

The Fifth Avenue Hotel in New York City installs the first passenger elevator in an American hotel.

Beginning of American Civil War.

President Lincoln proclaims the first national Thanksgiving Day, and sets aside the last Thursday of November to commemorate the great feast held by the Pilgrims in 1621.

Hecker's Self-Rising Flour, the first product of its kind, is produced by John and George Hecker.

Abraham Lincoln becomes the sixteenth president of the United States.

| 1846 | 1852 | 1859 | 1860 | 1861 | 1863 |

American Events

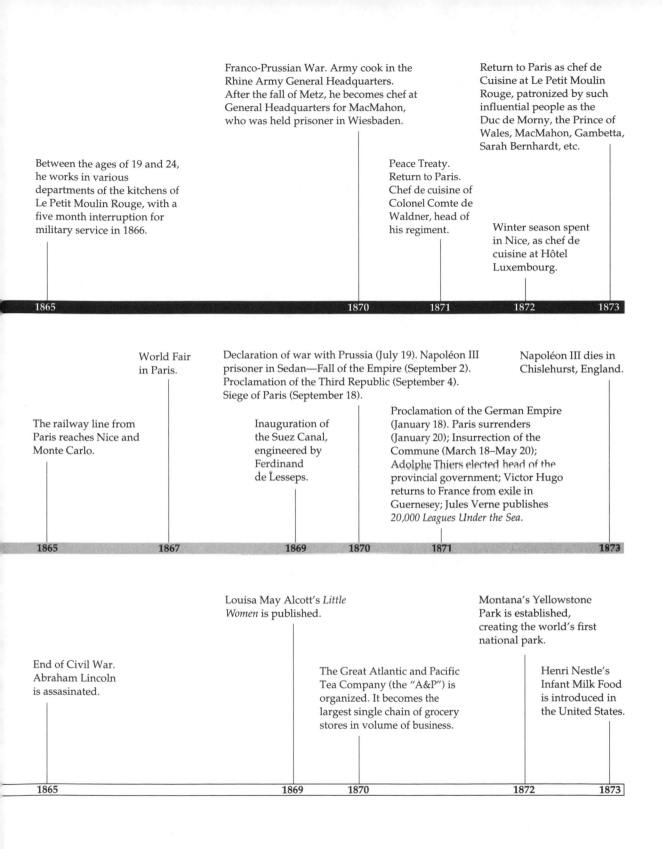

Timeline 1 (1865–1873)

Between the ages of 19 and 24, he works in various departments of the kitchens of Le Petit Moulin Rouge, with a five month interruption for military service in 1866.

Franco-Prussian War. Army cook in the Rhine Army General Headquarters. After the fall of Metz, he becomes chef at General Headquarters for MacMahon, who was held prisoner in Wiesbaden.

Peace Treaty. Return to Paris. Chef de cuisine of Colonel Comte de Waldner, head of his regiment.

Return to Paris as chef de Cuisine at Le Petit Moulin Rouge, patronized by such influential people as the Duc de Morny, the Prince of Wales, MacMahon, Gambetta, Sarah Bernhardt, etc.

Winter season spent in Nice, as chef de cuisine at Hôtel Luxembourg.

1865   1870   1871   1872   1873

Timeline 2 (1865–1873)

World Fair in Paris.

Declaration of war with Prussia (July 19). Napoléon III prisoner in Sedan—Fall of the Empire (September 2). Proclamation of the Third Republic (September 4). Siege of Paris (September 18).

Napoléon III dies in Chislehurst, England.

The railway line from Paris reaches Nice and Monte Carlo.

Inauguration of the Suez Canal, engineered by Ferdinand de Lesseps.

Proclamation of the German Empire (January 18). Paris surrenders (January 20); Insurrection of the Commune (March 18–May 20); Adolphe Thiers elected head of the provincial government; Victor Hugo returns to France from exile in Guernesey; Jules Verne publishes *20,000 Leagues Under the Sea*.

1865   1867   1869   1870   1871   1873

Timeline 3 (1865–1873)

Louisa May Alcott's *Little Women* is published.

Montana's Yellowstone Park is established, creating the world's first national park.

End of Civil War. Abraham Lincoln is assasinated.

The Great Atlantic and Pacific Tea Company (the "A&P") is organized. It becomes the largest single chain of grocery stores in volume of business.

Henri Nestle's Infant Milk Food is introduced in the United States.

1865   1869   1870   1872   1873

Escoffier opens his own restaurant in Cannes, Le Faisan Doré, sharing his time between Cannes and Paris.

Having left Le Petit Moulin Rouge, he takes on the management of La Maison Chevet, a famous caterer at the Palais Royale in Paris whose specialty is catering meals in various capitals of Europe.

Having established his reputation both as a cook and as a writer in the culinary world, Escoffier joins the Grand Hôtel in Monte Carlo as chef de cusine, at the invitation of César Ritz, the manager, and Mrs. Jungbluth, the owner. This is the beginning of a long-standing and mutually fruitful collaboration between the two men. Until 1888, they divide their time between the Grand Hôtel in Monte Carlo in the winter and the Hôtel National in Lucerne (Switzerland) in the summer.

In August, he marries Delphine Daffis, daughter of a prominent editor. They will have three children: Paul, Daniel, and Germaine.

Chef de cuisine at the Restaurant Maire in Paris, owned by Mr. Paillard.

Founding in Paris of the culinary magazine *L'Art Culinaire*.

| 1876 | 1878 | 1880 | 1881 | 1883 | 1884 |

Escoffier's Career

First exhibit of Impressionist painters.

Appearance of the first automobiles.

France in Madagascar and Indochina.

Opening of *Carmen*, opera written by George Bizet based on a short story by P. Mérimée.

World Fair in Paris.

French protectorate established in Tunisia. Beginning of the Panama Canal by F. de Lesseps.

Louis Pasteur invents the anti-rabies serum.

| 1874 | 1875 | 1878 | 1880 | 1881 | 1883 | 1885 |

World Events

Invention of the telephone by Alexander Graham Bell. The Centennial of the American Revolution.

Life magazine is established.

Edison invents the first practical electric incandescent lamp.

| 1876 | 1879 | 1883 |

American Events

Escoffier continues working in both hotels while Ritz leaves to manage a hotel in Baden-Baden and the Hôtel de Provence in Cannes.

Ritz takes over the management of the Savoy Hotel in London, a prestigious hotel built by d'Oyly Carte, and asks Escoffier to take over the management of the kitchen. The Savoy Hotel becomes the elegant meeting place of the international elite, the "jet-set society" of those times. The Duc d'Orléans, in exile, has his private apartments there, and the well-known opera singer Nellie Melba lives there in 1892–93.

For seven years, Escoffier serves the most famous people of the world, and creates his most renowned dishes. "Filets de sole Coquelin," "Homard aux feux éternels," "Volaille á la Derby," "Cuisses de nymphe á l'aurore," "Suprêmes de volaille Jeannette," and the celebrated "Pêche Melba."

Ritz creates the Ritz Development Company. Disagreements develop between him and the owners of the Savoy, and he resigns. Escoffier and the other managers of the hotel (Echenard, Agostini, and Henri Elles) follow him.

| 1888 | 1890 | 1897 |

Heinrich Hertz discovers electromagnetic wavelengths.

Edouard Branly invents the coherer, enabling wireless telegraphy. First motorized airplane (Clement Ader). First subway line in London. Beginning of the war in Sudan.

Emile Zola, studying poverty stricken neighborhoods in London, stays at the Savoy. First moving pictures: Cinématographe des Frères Lumière.

World Fair in Paris — the Eiffel Tower. First gasoline-run automobile (Daimler).

Franco-Russian Alliance.

Henri Becquerel discovers radioactivity. First modern Olympic Games created by Baron de Coubertin.

| 1887 | 1889 | 1890 | 1894 | 1895 | 1896 |

George Eastman perfects the Kodak hand-held camera, making amateur photography possible for the first time.

Jacob Riis's account of slum life, *How the Other Half Lives*, is published.

Fannie Farmer's *Boston Cooking School Cookbook* is published by Farmer, who has served as the cooking school's director since 1891.

First electrical tramway in the United States.

McCormick Spices has its beginnings in Baltimore, Maryland.

| 1887 | 1888 | 1889 | 1890 | 1896 |

June 5: Opening of the Hôtel Ritz, Place Vendôme, Paris, with Escoffier heading the kitchens, which he organizes entirely. The success of the Hôtel Ritz is immediate.

First publication of the *Guide Culinaire*, and founding of the Culinary Mutual Fund Association in London.

Return to London for the completion of the Carlton Hotel, its kitchens and restaurant. Ritz was to manage the hotel, which opened on July 1, with Escoffier in charge of the kitchens and the restaurant. His famous patrons follow from the Savoy. Escoffier stays at the Carlton until 1920, but Ritz, taken ill, has to retire in the early stages (1902).

Escoffier organizes the kitchens of the restaurants on board the liners of the Hamburg-Amerika Line, a major German shipping company.

| 1898 | 1899 | | | 1903 | 1904 |

Escoffier's Career

Pierre and Marie Curie discover radium. The Marchand Expedition in Sudan: conflict with Great Britain.

First subway line in Paris (Porte Maillot-Vincennes).

Edward VII crowned King of England.

The Dreyfus Affair.

Death of Queen Victoria in London.

Entente Cordiale between France and Great Britain.

| 1898 | 1899 | 1900 | 1901 | 1902 | 1904 |

World Events

Carry Nation, a temperance advocate, calls for the enactment of prohibition legislation.

Caloric Stove Corporation has its beginnings at the Caloric Stove Works in Philadelphia.

Horn and Hardart Baking Company's Automat, the first coin-operated automatic restaurant, opens in Philadelphia.

First Olympic Games held in the United States take place as part of the Exposition in St. Louis, Missouri.

| 1900 | 1902 | 1902 | 1904 |

American Events

In June, on board *Amerika*, first meeting with Wilhelm II, Emperor of Germany.

Professional Jubilee in honor of Escoffier, who requests that the amount collected for his gift be donated to the home for retired chefs.

Founding in London of the magazine *Le Carnet d'Epicure*. Great fire at the Carlton. Escoffier narrowly escapes, unhurt.

Second meeting with Kaiser Wilhelm II, on board *Imperator*, flagship of the Hamburg-Amerika Line, during her maiden cruise.

First trip to the United States.

Publication of an essay on the benefit of mutual assistance to suppress poverty. Second trip to the United States for the opening of the Ritz-Carlton in New York.

Publication of *Livre des Menus*.

Great activity at the Carlton. Escoffier forms a committee to help the families of chefs drafted in France.

| 1906 | 1907 | 1909 | 1910 | 1911 | 1912 | 1913 | 1914 |

Beginning of World War I (August 3). Opening of the Panama Canal. First transatlantic radiotelephone communication is sent between Arlington, Virginia, and the Eiffel Tower in Paris.

Armistice Day (November 11).

Louis Blériot is the first to fly across the English Channel (July 25).

French protectorate established in Morocco. Sinking of the *Titanic*.

Bolshevik revolution in Russia — Lenin imposes communism.

| 1909 | 1912 | 1914 | 1917 | 1918 |

Pure Food and Drug Act prohibits the sale of adulterated (impure) foods and drugs, and requires disclosure of contents on product labels.

Invention of air conditioning.

There are 4.8 million motor vehicles registered in the United States. Average price of a new car is $750.

First fleet of metered taxicabs, imported from Paris, arrives in New York City.

The Armory Show, the first major American twentieth century international art exhibition, is held in New York City.

| 1906 | 1907 | 1911 | 1913 | 1917 |

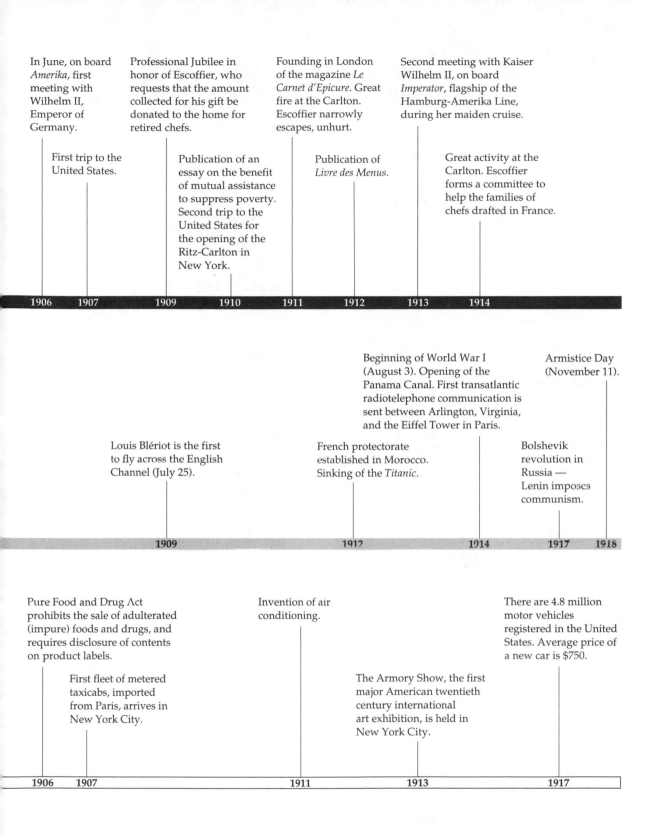

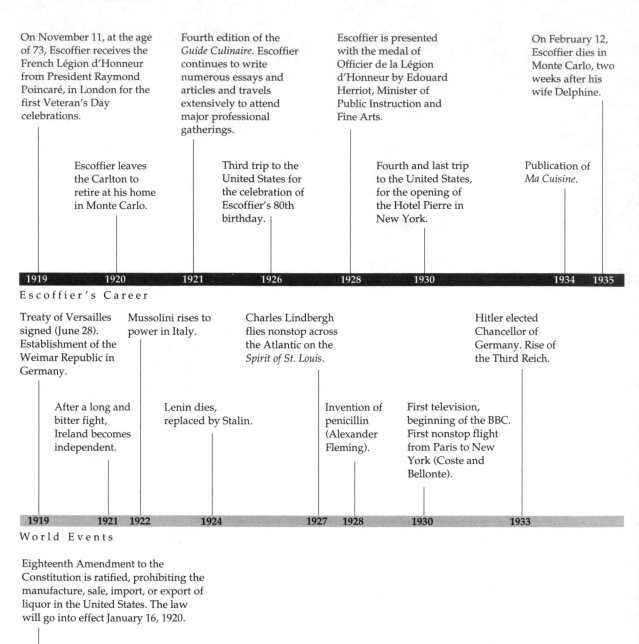

On November 11, at the age of 73, Escoffier receives the French Légion d'Honneur from President Raymond Poincaré, in London for the first Veteran's Day celebrations.

Fourth edition of the *Guide Culinaire*. Escoffier continues to write numerous essays and articles and travels extensively to attend major professional gatherings.

Escoffier is presented with the medal of Officier de la Légion d'Honneur by Edouard Herriot, Minister of Public Instruction and Fine Arts.

On February 12, Escoffier dies in Monte Carlo, two weeks after his wife Delphine.

Escoffier leaves the Carlton to retire at his home in Monte Carlo.

Third trip to the United States for the celebration of Escoffier's 80th birthday.

Fourth and last trip to the United States, for the opening of the Hotel Pierre in New York.

Publication of *Ma Cuisine*.

| 1919 | 1920 | 1921 | 1926 | 1928 | 1930 | 1934 | 1935 |

Escoffier's Career

Treaty of Versailles signed (June 28). Establishment of the Weimar Republic in Germany.

Mussolini rises to power in Italy.

Charles Lindbergh flies nonstop across the Atlantic on the *Spirit of St. Louis*.

Hitler elected Chancellor of Germany. Rise of the Third Reich.

After a long and bitter fight, Ireland becomes independent.

Lenin dies, replaced by Stalin.

Invention of penicillin (Alexander Fleming).

First television, beginning of the BBC. First nonstop flight from Paris to New York (Coste and Bellonte).

| 1919 | 1921 | 1922 | 1924 | 1927 | 1928 | 1930 | 1933 |

World Events

Eighteenth Amendment to the Constitution is ratified, prohibiting the manufacture, sale, import, or export of liquor in the United States. The law will go into effect January 16, 1920.

Women get the vote when the Nineteenth Amendment to the Contitution is ratified. F. Scott Fitzgerald publishes *This Side of Paradise*, helping to initiate "the Jazz Age."

First speaking movies (MGM). The Stock Market crashes, initiating a series of crises that will result in worldwide economic depression.

| 1919 | 1920 | 1929 |

American Events

Index